5 STEPS TO A >5™

500

AP Human Geography
Questions

to know by test day

5 STEPS TO A >5™

500
AP Human Geography Questions
to know by test day

SECOND EDITION

Anaxos, Inc.

New York Chicago San Francisco Athens London Madrid
Mexico City Milan New Delhi Singapore Sydney Toronto

Anaxos, Inc. (Austin, TX) has been creating education and reference materials for over fifteen years. Based in Austin, Texas, the company uses writers from across the globe who offer expertise on an array of subjects just as expansive.

1 2 3 4 5 6 7 8 9   QFR   21 20 19 18 17 16

ISBN   978-1-259-83671-8
MHID   1-259-83671-1

e-ISBN   978-1-259-83672-5
e-MHID   1-259-83672-X

McGraw-Hill Education, the McGraw-Hill Education logo, 5 Steps to a 5, and related trade dress are trademarks or registered trademarks of McGraw-Hill Education and/or its affiliates in the United States and other countries and may not be used without written permission. All other trademarks are the property of their respective owners. McGraw-Hill Education is not associated with any product or vendor mentioned in this book.

AP, *Advanced Placement Program*, and *College Board* are registered trademarks of the College Board, which was not involved in the production of, and does not endorse, this product.

McGraw-Hill Education products are available at special quantity discounts to use as premiums and sales promotions or for use in corporate training programs. To contact a representative, please visit the Contact Us pages at www.mhprofessional.com.

CONTENTS

INTRODUCTION

Congratulations! You've taken a big step toward AP success by purchasing *5 Steps to a 5: 500 AP Human Geography Questions to Know by Test Day*. We are here to help you take the next step and score high on your AP Exam so you can earn college credits and get into the college or university of your choice.

This book gives you 500 AP-style multiple-choice questions that cover all the most essential course material, in addition to short essay questions at the end of each chapter similar to those on the AP exam. Each question has a detailed answer explanation that can be found at the back of the book. These questions will give you valuable independent practice to supplement your regular textbook and the groundwork you are already doing in your AP classroom. This and the other books in this series were written by expert AP teachers who know your exam inside and out and can identify the crucial exam information as well as questions that are most likely to appear on the test.

You might be the kind of student who takes several AP courses and needs to study extra questions a few weeks before the exam for a final review. Or you might be the kind of student who puts off preparing until the last weeks before the exam. No matter what your preparation style is, you will surely benefit from reviewing these 500 questions, which closely parallel the content, format, and degree of difficulty of the questions on the actual AP Exam. These questions and their answer explanations are the ideal last-minute study tool for those final few weeks before the test.

Remember the old saying "Practice makes perfect." If you practice with all the questions and answers in this book, we are certain you will build the skills and confidence needed to do great on the exam. Good luck!

—Editors of McGraw-Hill Education

5 STEPS TO A 5™

500
AP Human Geography Questions
to know by test day

CHAPTER 1

Key Geography Concepts

1. A ratio of the number of items within a defined unit of area measures
   (A) dispersion
   (B) direction
   (C) pattern
   (D) density
   (E) diffusion

2. Which of the following best describes the *site* of Manhattan?
   (A) A regional transportation hub for the northeastern United States
   (B) A midway point along an urban corridor stretching from Boston to Washington, DC
   (C) An island bordered by the Hudson and East Rivers
   (D) An important center for international trade and commerce
   (E) An urban center located two hours northeast of Philadelphia by train

3. Spatial coordinates of latitude and longitude express
   (A) relative location
   (B) absolute location
   (C) relative direction
   (D) absolute direction
   (E) relative distance

4. Which of the following concepts refers to the spatial arrangement of items or features within a given area?
   (A) Distribution
   (B) Direction
   (C) Accessibility
   (D) Trajectory
   (E) Scale

5. A method for representing the three-dimensional surface of the earth on the two-dimensional surface of a map is known as
   (A) scale
   (B) globalization
   (C) proximity
   (D) ethnography
   (E) projection

6. A subjective image of an area informed by individual perceptions and experiences in that area is known as a
   (A) thematic map
   (B) reference map
   (C) mental map
   (D) contour map
   (E) topographic map

7. The notion that the physical environment offers certain constraints and opportunities that influence cultural practices without entirely determining them is known as
   (A) assimilation
   (B) possibilism
   (C) diffusion
   (D) determinism
   (E) divergence

8. Which of the following is NOT true of culture?
   (A) It is biologically inherited.
   (B) It varies from place to place.
   (C) It can converge and diverge over time.
   (D) It can diffuse across space.
   (E) It expresses human adaptations and innovations.

9. Which of the following phenomena most directly illustrates the concept of cultural convergence?
   (A) Linguistic drift
   (B) Ethnic separatism
   (C) Globalization
   (D) Gerrymandering
   (E) Religious fundamentalism

10. The idea that material innovations, such as new technologies, diffuse more rapidly than newly exposed cultures can adequately respond and adapt to them best illustrates the idea of
    (A) cultural divergence
    (B) stimulus diffusion
    (C) environmental determinism
    (D) cultural lag
    (E) relocation diffusion

11. The principle of distance decay describes
    (A) a positive correlation between distance and degree of relation
    (B) a neutral correlation between distance and degree of relation
    (C) a negative correlation between distance and degree of relation
    (D) an uncertain correlation between distance and degree of relation
    (E) no correlation between distance and degree of relation

12. The particular conditions that compel individuals or groups to migrate from one place to another are commonly referred to as
    (A) cause and effect issues
    (B) place and space dynamics
    (C) local and global conflicts
    (D) past and future concerns
    (E) push and pull factors

13. Economic and/or political associations that are comprised of multiple, autonomous member states that cooperate to achieve a common purpose are known as
    (A) transnational corporations
    (B) supranational organizations
    (C) multiethnic societies
    (D) nationalism
    (E) nongovernmental organizations

14. Which of the following U.S. cities is a site along the Mississippi River and is situated as a major port for offshore petroleum production in the Gulf of Mexico?
    (A) St. Louis
    (B) Houston
    (C) Mobile
    (D) New Orleans
    (E) Minneapolis

15. The ability to travel and communicate over greater distances in shorter amounts of time, due to technological innovations such as the airplane, automobile, telephone, and Internet, represents the idea of
    (A) time-space compression
    (B) stimulus diffusion
    (C) friction of distance
    (D) relocation diffusion
    (E) possibilism

16. Which of the following cartographic terms describes the location of a place in terms of its angular distance north or south of the equator?
    (A) Longitude
    (B) Azimuth
    (C) Latitude
    (D) Meridian
    (E) Legend

17. During the process of mapmaking, in which the three-dimensional surface of the earth is projected onto a flat, two-dimensional surface, all of the following attributes can become distorted EXCEPT
    (A) shape
    (B) area
    (C) distance
    (D) direction
    (E) relative location

18. The Prime Meridian, which passes through Greenwich, England, is equivalent to which of the following lines of longitude?

    (A) 0° longitude
    (B) 45° longitude
    (C) 90° longitude
    (D) 180° longitude
    (E) 270° longitude

19. The geographical region whose center is located along the equator and whose area extends roughly 23° north and south of the equator is known as the

    (A) polar region
    (B) tundra
    (C) rainforest region
    (D) tropical zone
    (E) taiga

20. Which of the following terms refers to a ratio between distances portrayed on a map and actual distances on the earth's surface that correspond to this map?

    (A) Chart
    (B) Scale
    (C) Contour
    (D) Grid
    (E) Projection

21. Processes of globalization are most closely associated with which of the following forms of socioeconomic organization?

    (A) Mutualism
    (B) Socialism
    (C) Feudalism
    (D) Capitalism
    (E) Communism

22. A subfield of geography that deals holistically with the environmental and human attributes of a particular territory is known as
    (A) human geography
    (B) political geography
    (C) physical geography
    (D) biogeography
    (E) regional geography

23. Which of the following terms most directly refers to geographical techniques that collect information about the earth's surface from distantiated perspectives?
    (A) Geographic information systems
    (B) Geomancy
    (C) Remote sensing
    (D) Ethnography
    (E) Demography

24. What type of diffusion best describes when a characteristic begins to spread through a population from people in authority?
    (A) Contagious
    (B) Stimulus
    (C) Hierarchical
    (D) Ethnic
    (E) Relocation

25. In the context of the contemporary United States, a strip mall shopping center best exemplifies which of the following types of landscape?
    (A) Ordinary landscape
    (B) Sacred landscape
    (C) Tragic landscape
    (D) Derelict landscape
    (E) Industrial landscape

26. The forced dispersion of Jews from their ethnic homeland, which took place across many centuries, is a prominent example of
    (A) stimulus diffusion
    (B) diaspora
    (C) pilgrimage
    (D) globalization
    (E) receptivity

27. Which of the following best describes the *site* of Mexico City?
    (A) The most important financial and political center in Mexico
    (B) An urban area located approximately two hours from Houston, Texas, by airplane
    (C) A highland valley and dry lakebed located on a high plateau in southern central Mexico
    (D) The federal district of Mexico
    (E) An important node in a global system of flows of goods, information, and people

28. Which of the following examples best illustrates the concept of cognitive distance?
    (A) Distance expressed in terms of the amount of money it costs to travel from one place to another
    (B) Distance measured in terms of miles or kilometers
    (C) Distance measured in terms of minutes or hours
    (D) Distance expressed in terms of the perceived amount of space separating one place from another
    (E) Distance expressed in terms of how far the average person can walk in one day

29. In cartography, parallels refer to
    (A) lines of latitude
    (B) meridians
    (C) the scale of the map
    (D) lines of longitude
    (E) the alignment of the poles

30. Which of the following examples is least likely to be perceived as a path in cognitive space?
    (A) A navigable river
    (B) An interstate highway
    (C) A running trail
    (D) A sidewalk
    (E) An impenetrable forest

31. Which of the following is NOT an example of a vernacular region?
    (A) The Rust Belt
    (B) Kansas
    (C) The Deep South
    (D) The Jersey Shore
    (E) The Amazon

32. Thematic maps that employ a range of color tones to illustrate how particular values vary across predefined areas, such as counties, provinces, or states, are referred to as
    (A) dot maps
    (B) choropleth maps
    (C) proportional symbol maps
    (D) isoline maps
    (E) cartograms

33. Curves on a topographic map that are used to illustrate specific values of elevation above or below sea level are known as
    (A) district lines
    (B) latitudinal lines
    (C) transmission lines
    (D) contour lines
    (E) longitudinal lines

34. A travel agency surveys 100 adults in the local area regarding their travel habits. Among the findings, the travel agency discovers that 90 percent of survey participants indicate that they are willing to travel between 100 and 200 miles to attend a family reunion. However, beyond a distance of 200 miles, the percentage of survey participants willing to travel to a family reunion plummets to under 30 percent. Within this context, the change in willingness to travel demonstrates what concept?

   (A) Pull factor
   (B) Critical distance
   (C) Intervening opportunity
   (D) Push factor
   (E) Regional bias

35. Map projections that preserve and accurately represent the *shape* of the geographical areas and features are said to be

   (A) conformal
   (B) equidistant
   (C) equal-area
   (D) azimuthal
   (E) useless

36. Which of the following geometric map projections would be most appropriate for producing a world map in which the equatorial zone is least distorted?

   (A) Cylindrical
   (B) Conical
   (C) Planar
   (D) Azimuthal
   (E) Pseudoconical

37. The cardinal points north, east, south, and west correspond to

   (A) relative location
   (B) absolute distance
   (C) absolute location
   (D) relative distance
   (E) absolute direction

38. Which of the following fields of study is *least associated* with human geography?
    (A) Psychology
    (B) Cultural ecology
    (C) Sociology
    (D) Geomorphology
    (E) Political science

39. *Accessibility* and *connectivity* are two interrelated ways to describe
    (A) absolute locations
    (B) spatial concentrations
    (C) relative directions
    (D) geographical sites
    (E) spatial interactions

40. Relative to the lines of longitude near the equator, the lines of longitude near the poles are
    (A) longer
    (B) closer together
    (C) shorter
    (D) wider
    (E) more accurate

41. The geographical concept of a *network* is an important tool in human geography for describing complex spatial interactions, particularly those that have been created or modified by globalization.
    (A) Define a network.
    (B) Briefly explain how each of the following four terms relate to the concept of a network: *mobility, diffusion, interdependence,* and *situation.*
    (C) Briefly explain why networks are particularly relevant tools for describing spatial interactions in a globalized era. Cite two real-world examples to help illustrate your explanation.

42. The concept of *placelessness* was coined in human geography in the 1970s to describe places that feel inauthentic or lack a unique sense of identity. Many geographers theorize that a sense of placelessness is becoming more prevalent among people living in modern, highly developed societies. Discuss how each of the following has contributed to this sense of placelessness in developed societies.

    (A) Popular culture
    (B) Industrialization
    (C) Globalization
    (D) Mobility

CHAPTER 2

Population

43. An example of a country with a population pyramid that has a large base is

(A) Japan
(B) Germany
(C) Nigeria
(D) United States
(E) Russia

44. The demographic transition model suggests that as countries industrialize

(A) in-migration increases over time
(B) migration increases from rural to urban areas
(C) birth and death rates decrease over time
(D) life expectancy decreases over time
(E) fertility rates increase over time

45. The first stage of the demographic transition model indicates that

(A) total population is low and constant with high birth rates and low death rates
(B) total population is low and constant with low birth rates and high death rates
(C) total population is increasing with high birth rates and low death rates
(D) total population is low and constant with high birth rates and high death rates
(E) total population is low and constant with low birth rates and low death rates

46. Which of the following is NOT a contributing factor to the low birth rates in stage four of the demographic transition model?
    (A) Less dependence on child labor
    (B) Reliance on subsistence agriculture
    (C) The education of women
    (D) Availability of health care
    (E) Increased sanitation

47. According to Thomas Malthus's population theory, which of the following is a preventive check on population?
    (A) Famine
    (B) Disease
    (C) War
    (D) Moral restraint
    (E) Disaster

48. Which of the following population control examples did Thomas Malthus support?
    (A) The upper class utilizing moral restraint to limit family size
    (B) The upper class paying additional taxes to fund family planning and cleanliness education for the lower class
    (C) Equitably distributing food among all citizens regardless of wealth during times of famine
    (D) Relocating cities and towns away from stagnant pools and marshy lands to promote better health among all citizens
    (E) Widening city streets in low-income neighborhoods to reduce overcrowding and the spread of disease

49. Which of the following countries contains the most cities with populations above 10 million?
    (A) Brazil
    (B) United States
    (C) China
    (D) India
    (E) Mexico

50. China's one-child policy is an example of what concept?

    (A) Maximum population theory
    (B) Ideal population theory
    (C) Optimum population policy
    (D) Select population theory
    (E) Pro-natalist government policy

51. Which of the following is NOT a result of overpopulation?

    (A) Squatter settlements in Rio de Janeiro
    (B) Low unemployment rates in Tokyo
    (C) Deforestation in Madagascar
    (D) Overcrowding in Mumbai
    (E) Lack of access to food in Manila

52. Which of the following regions has the highest rate of natural increase?

    (A) Sub-Saharan Africa
    (B) North America
    (C) Australia
    (D) Europe
    (E) Russian Domain

53. Arithmetic population density can be calculated by

    (A) total land area multiplied by total population
    (B) total land area minus total population
    (C) total population multiplied by total land area
    (D) total population minus total population
    (E) total population divided by total land area

54. In the United States suburbanization increased in the 1960s and resulted in which of the following?

    (A) Loss of tax base and increased poverty rates in city centers
    (B) Renovation of city centers and increased employment opportunities
    (C) Improved race relations through gentrification
    (D) High unemployment rates in the suburbs as jobs remained downtown
    (E) Increased use of public transportation

55. Commercial farming led to what 20th-century population change in North America?

(A) Urban decentralization
(B) The growth of the Sunbelt
(C) Counterurbanization
(D) Rural-to-urban migration
(E) The "black exodus" from the South

56. Which of the following cities is an example of urban primacy?

(A) Los Angeles
(B) Buenos Aires
(C) Toronto
(D) Moscow
(E) Rome

57. The population of developed nations can be described as having

(A) higher fertility rates than less developed countries
(B) higher crude death rates than less developed countries
(C) higher crude birth rates than less developed countries
(D) lower natural increase than less developed countries
(E) lower life expectancy rates than less developed countries

58. Between 1990 and 1999, population increased in the United States due primarily to which factor?

(A) Increased immigration
(B) Decreased emigration
(C) Increased birth rate
(D) Decreased death rate
(E) Increased fertility rates

59. Food availability, which can control population size, is an example of a

(A) control factor
(B) supply factor
(C) regulating factor
(D) limiting factor
(E) managing factor

60. In general, which of the following is true about carrying capacity and population?
    (A) Above carrying capacity, population size increases.
    (B) Above carrying capacity, population size decreases.
    (C) Above carrying capacity, population size remains constant.
    (D) Below carrying capacity, population size decreases.
    (E) Below carrying capacity, population size remains constant.

61. In order for doubling time to be accurately predicted, which of the following assumptions must be true?
    (A) That the population growth rate fluctuates annually
    (B) That the population growth rate is decreasing annually
    (C) That the population growth rate is constant over a long period of time
    (D) That the population growth rate is increasing over a long period of time
    (E) That the population growth rate is cyclic over a long period of time

62. The age-specific fertility rate (ASFR) among women in the United States from 1955 to 1995 indicates that
    (A) women are having more children and starting families earlier in life
    (B) women are having more children and starting families later in life
    (C) women are having fewer children and starting families earlier in life
    (D) women are having fewer children and starting families later in life
    (E) there is no change in timing or child birth rates during this time period

63. For an emigrant, war in his or her homeland is an example of a
    (A) push factor
    (B) draw factor
    (C) pull factor
    (D) force factor
    (E) driving factor

64. Baby booms are generally associated with

    (A) periods of economic hardship
    (B) increased education of women
    (C) periods of economic prosperity
    (D) increased number of women in the workforce
    (E) times of war

65. The primary purpose of demographic data is to

    (A) predict future migration patterns of a population
    (B) describe the characteristics of a population
    (C) estimate population density of a nation
    (D) identify when a population will reach its carrying capacity
    (E) calculate population decline of a nation

66. A high dependency ratio suggests that a large percentage of the population is

    (A) between 14 and 64 years old
    (B) 65 years or older
    (C) under 14 years old
    (D) under 14 years old and over 65 years old
    (E) between 1 and 64 years old

67. Which of the following is true regarding older populations in developed countries?

    (A) Men tend to outlive women.
    (B) Older populations vote less than younger populations.
    (C) The older population growth is slower than the younger population growth.
    (D) Older men are less likely to be married than older women.
    (E) The majority of older people are women.

68. Which of the following countries has the lowest life expectancy at birth?

    (A) Zimbabwe
    (B) Japan
    (C) Chile
    (D) Switzerland
    (E) Canada

69. The act of migrants sending money to family in their home country is termed

(A) alimony
(B) allowance
(C) subsidence
(D) remittance
(E) restitution

70. Generation X, which is a group of individuals all born within a defined time interval, is an example of a

(A) unit
(B) cohort
(C) class
(D) brigade
(E) division

71. A temporary and notable increase in the birth rate is called a

(A) birth dearth
(B) population surge
(C) baby boom
(D) mortality event
(E) pro-natalist policy

72. A population continuing to grow following a fertility decline due to the large percentage of young people is known as

(A) demographic thrust
(B) demographic push
(C) demographic surge
(D) demographic force
(E) demographic momentum

73. Influenza is an example of which type of disease diffusion?

(A) Network
(B) Relocation
(C) Hierarchical
(D) Contagious
(E) Mixed

74. The term *ecumene* refers to

(A) the amount of time it takes a population to double in size

(B) the amount of land that is inhabited by humans

(C) regions under environmental stress due to overpopulation

(D) the distribution of goods and services within a population

(E) the number of farmers per unit area of farmland

75. Neo-Malthusian theory builds on Malthus's overpopulation theory by considering which two additional factors?

(A) Population growth of developing countries and the outstripping of other resources beyond food

(B) Population growth of developing countries and the invention of new technologies to provide necessary resources

(C) Population growth of developing countries and the population decline of developed countries

(D) Population decline of developed countries and the outstripping of other resources beyond food

(E) Population decline of developed countries and the invention of new technologies to provide necessary resources

76. A nomadic tribe that migrates seasonally to follow the availability of plants and game is an example of

(A) repeated migration

(B) chain migration

(C) recurrent movement

(D) temporary movement

(E) cyclic movement

77. The gravity model predicts

(A) the number of people a city can support with available resources

(B) the rate at which intercontinental migration occurs

(C) the movement of people, goods, and ideas between two locations based on size and distance

(D) periods of population explosion in a certain geographic region

(E) the physiological density of a country

78. The seasonal migration of livestock between lowlands and mountains is termed

    (A) step migration
    (B) transmigration
    (C) periodic movement
    (D) transhumance
    (E) interregional migration

79. A husband migrates from Mexico to the United States and earns money to allow for his family to follow him to the United States. This is an example of

    (A) chain migration
    (B) forced migration
    (C) distance decay
    (D) internal migration
    (E) interregional migration

80. Which of the following is true regarding fertility differentials in the United States in 2017?

    (A) Metropolitan areas experience higher rates of fertility than rural areas.
    (B) Fertility rates are highest among low-income groups.
    (C) Women with college degrees have higher fertility rates than high school–educated women.
    (D) Women aged 16–20 have the highest fertility rates of any age group.
    (E) Hispanic women have lower fertility rates than white women.

81. To compensate for growing populations, developing countries have tried to raise the crop yields of existing farmland by

    (A) decreasing irrigation
    (B) using manure instead of chemical fertilizers
    (C) planting genetically modified plants that produce more food per acre
    (D) finding new land to farm
    (E) reducing their dependency on pesticides

82. Which regions have the fewest freshwater resources per capita?

    (A) Latin America and the Caribbean
    (B) Europe and Central Asia
    (C) Middle East and North Africa
    (D) Sub-Saharan Africa and South Asia
    (E) East Asia and the Pacific

83. Which of the following countries has the least arable land per capita?

    (A) Canada
    (B) Argentina
    (C) Australia
    (D) Kazakhstan
    (E) China

84. The process where voting districts are spatially altered to favor one political party over another is known as

    (A) repositioning
    (B) gerrymandering
    (C) reapportionment
    (D) packing
    (E) riding

85. The Homestead Act of 1862, which governed the initial settlement of the Great Plains, resulted in which rural population spatial pattern?

    (A) Random
    (B) Clustered
    (C) Uniform
    (D) Unsystematic
    (E) Erratic

86. Factors that prevent a species from reproducing at its maximum rate are known as environmental

    (A) fecundity
    (B) fertility
    (C) struggle
    (D) limits
    (E) resistance

87. The maximum reproductive capacity of a population is known as

(A) sterility
(B) fertility
(C) fruitful
(D) fecundity
(E) prolific

88. Population distribution that is evenly spread over a landscape typically in low densities is called

(A) concentrated distribution
(B) dispersed distribution
(C) scattered distribution
(D) condensed distribution
(E) diluted distribution

89. Gross national product (GNP) per capita is the

(A) total value of produced goods and services of a country in one year divided by total number of people living in the country
(B) total value of produced goods and services of a country in one year multiplied by total number of people living in the country
(C) total number of people living in the country divided by the total value of produced goods and services of a country in one year
(D) total number of people living in the country minus the total value of produced goods and services of a country in one year
(E) total value of produced goods and services of a country in one year minus the total number of people living in the country

90. In some countries, a foreign person who is given temporary permission to live and work in a host country is known as a

(A) guest worker
(B) temporary laborer
(C) host laborer
(D) interim worker
(E) provisional laborer

91. The rule of 70 is used to measure

(A) the goal life expectancy for developing countries

(B) the percentage of people living above extreme poverty levels

(C) the approximate amount of time it takes for a population to double

(D) the literacy rate in developed countries

(E) the average growing period for subsistence farming in developing countries

92. Which of the following is an example of a choropleth map?

(A) A map with distorted areas that reflect varying GNPs and not the size and shape of the country

(B) A birth-rate map that uses different colors to represent countries with varying birth rates

(C) A map using arrows to indicate the global flow of commodities

(D) A population map that uses dots to represent population density

(E) A crop yield map that uses isolines to connect areas with the same crop yields

93. Malaria, which is present in many populations living in tropical or subtropical regions, is an example of a(n)

(A) epidemic

(B) endodermic

(C) pandemic

(D) prosodemic

(E) endemic disease

94. Which of the following is true regarding standard of living?

(A) Standard of living indicates the percentage of the population that is malnourished.

(B) Standard of living reflects the age distribution of a country.

(C) Standard of living is a measure of a country's GNP.

(D) Standard of living can trace development of a country.

(E) Standard of living is a direct result of the literacy rate of a country.

95. A J-curve on a population graph indicates

(A) exponential population growth
(B) cyclical population growth
(C) negative population growth
(D) quadratic function
(E) linear population growth

96. Which of the following is true regarding least developed countries (LDC) and most developed countries (MDC)?

(A) LDC have lower infant mortality rates than MDC.
(B) LDC have higher standards of living than MDC.
(C) MDC have higher literacy rates than LDC.
(D) Economies of MDC have more reliance on agricultural production than LDC.
(E) LDC have higher gross national incomes (GNI) than MDC.

97. A factor that persuades an immigrant to settle en route to his or her planned destination is called a(n)

(A) interfering factor
(B) intervening opportunity
(C) interruption
(D) interceding factor
(E) disrupting opportunity

98. A country that has high development levels, innovation capacity, and a convergence of trade flows is known as a(n)

(A) interior country
(B) central country
(C) periphery country
(D) primary country
(E) core country

99. Panama is classified as a periphery country due to which of the following factors?

(A) Panama is a least developed country and has a low GNP.

(B) Panama has a geographic location far from the Old World countries.

(C) Panama has low immigration rates.

(D) Panama is considered a frontier that is sparsely inhabited.

(E) Panama has many ports and trade routes that enable a high flow of goods and services.

100. Which of the following is NOT one of Ravenstein's migration laws?

(A) Most migration is rural to urban.

(B) Migrants traveling long distances will likely settle in a big city.

(C) People in rural areas are more migratory than city dwellers.

(D) Most international migrants are young women.

(E) Most migration is step migration.

101. What is the point when a country enters the fifth stage of the Demographic Transition Model?

(A) The immigration rate is higher than the birth rate.

(B) More people are migrating out of the country than are immigrating.

(C) Urban dwellers outnumber people living in rural communities.

(D) The country is experiencing counter migration.

(E) The birth rate is lower than the death rate.

102. All of the following are examples of forced migration EXCEPT

(A) the Trail of Tears in the early 19th century

(B) the Atlantic slave trade

(C) the California gold rush in the mid-19th century

(D) the Irish Potato Famine from 1846 to 1850

(E) the Japanese internment camps during World War II

103. The phenomenon where highly educated, intelligent, or professional people are more likely to migrate than other groups is an example of

(A) birth dearth

(B) irregular migration

(C) brain drain

(D) impelled migration

(E) seasonal migration

104. Which of the following is true regarding emigration?

(A) Emigration results in an influx of talented people in underdeveloped countries.

(B) Emigration reduces the pressure on land in overpopulated areas.

(C) Emigration increases unemployment rates in underdeveloped countries.

(D) Emigration can speed up development in underpopulated areas.

(E) Emigration can increase culture diversity.

105. The practice of harvesting crops twice a year, thus resulting in poor soil quality, is known as

(A) double cropping

(B) repeat planting

(C) crop replication

(D) duplicate planting

(E) twofold cropping

106. Several families living close together in multiple houses surrounded by farms is termed

(A) clustered

(B) dispersed

(C) nucleated

(D) bundled

(E) bunched

107. A refugee is defined as a person

(A) who willingly left his or her homeland for better opportunities in another country

(B) who illegally resides in a country other than his or her homeland

(C) who works outside of his or her home country

(D) who flees their home country due to war or persecution

(E) who was deported from a country back to his or her homeland

108. Which of the following is a consequence of negative population growth?

(A) Higher rates of malnutrition

(B) Reduced strain on available resources

(C) A larger workforce

(D) Increased fertility rates

(E) Decreased progress toward development in least developed countries

109. What is a contributing factor to the unbalanced sex ratio in some South and East Asian countries?

(A) Female infanticide

(B) The HIV epidemic

(C) Decreased government spending on health care

(D) Pro-natalist government policies

(E) Increased maternal mortalities

110. In a developed country, all of the following are likely to lower the rate of natural increase (RNI) of the population EXCEPT

(A) women gaining political and economic rights

(B) very high divorce rates

(C) a proliferation of single-parent, single-child families

(D) a high rate of immigration

(E) a high number of DINK (double-income, no kids) households

111. All of the following are true of the total fertility rate (TFR) equation EXCEPT

(A) A large population must have a TFR of 2.1 in order to replace itself.

(B) The TFR equation calculates average number of children born per woman of birthing age (15 to 45).

(C) TFR, like RNI, can be negative.

(D) A country with a low TFR may still experience a growing population.

(E) The TFR is a synthetic number, not based on the actual fertility of any group.

112. Which of the following characteristics is NOT true of a country in Stage 1 of demographic transition?

(A) High birth rate
(B) High death rate
(C) High infant mortality
(D) Slow population growth
(E) An industrial-based economy

113. All of the following are arguments advanced by neo-Malthusians with regard to future world population growth EXCEPT

(A) Global food demand will rise as third-world countries develop.
(B) Technological advancements will likely solve issues of food production and consumption.
(C) Current environmental problems could keep food-producing regions of the world from producing comparable amounts in the future.
(D) Overconsumption of other resources like coal and timber will not be sustainable as population increases.
(E) Even if global population numbers level off over the next several decades, a myriad of issues will still confront the world community.

114. Which of the following might account for the triangle-shaped population graph of the city of Brownsville in southern Texas?

(A) A large population of retirees moving from colder cities in the northeast
(B) A large college-age population
(C) Very low birth rates due to an inflow of young professionals
(D) Large numbers of Mexican immigrants, causing the graph to be similar to that of Mexico
(E) A much larger population of men than women

115. Migration in which people move to a series of increasingly more economically advantageous locations is referred to as

(A) step migration
(B) forced migration
(C) cyclic movement
(D) periodic movement
(E) demographic transition

116. All of the following are potential pull factors for immigration EXCEPT

(A) access to health-care services

(B) the high cost of land

(C) potential for higher-paying employment

(D) access to electricity and utilities

(E) entertainment options like television and sports

117. Which of the following best describes the general direction that the population center of the United States has moved since 1790?

(A) North and east

(B) South

(C) West and south

(D) North and west

(E) South and east

118. All of the following are true of physiologic density EXCEPT

(A) Unlike arithmetic density, physiologic density calculates number of people per unit of farmland.

(B) Countries like Iraq, Egypt, and Uzbekistan have high physiologic densities because the amount of arable land is low.

(C) Physiologic density helps illustrate why in the United States populations have moved to urban areas and into the western part of the country.

(D) Physiologic density is useful in determining the sustainability of a population in a given region.

(E) A country with a high physiologic density must also have a high arithmetic density.

119. Chronic diseases are more common today than in the past in developed countries due to

(A) better health care

(B) longer life expectancies

(C) decreased malnutrition

(D) population decline

(E) increased access to clean water

120. All of the following accurately reflect the attitudes of Thomas Malthus toward the poor EXCEPT
   (A) Wealthy people giving money to the poor would deprive the world of culture and refinement.
   (B) Preventive checks were not enough to control the population of the poor.
   (C) Better health care and sanitation should not be provided to poor people.
   (D) A surplus population of poor people was necessary to provide a stable workforce.
   (E) Left unchecked, the population of poor people would be ultimately limited by famine.

121. In 1977 Abdel Omran first described the epidemiological transition model that explains health and disease patterns in populations.
   (A) Identify and explain how the three major stages of the epidemiological transition model impact population growth, life expectancy, and mortality rates at each stage.
   (B) Identify and explain two factors (either social, environmental, or economic) that contribute to longer life expectancies at birth.

122. Stouffer's law of intervening opportunities (1940) suggests that migration is the result of the available opportunities and NOT distance as suggested by the gravity model.
   (A) Define a migration push factor and provide two examples.
   (B) Define an intervening opportunity and provide two examples.
   (C) Define a migration pull factor and provide two examples.

CHAPTER 3

Culture

123. In which of the following countries is one most likely to find speakers whose native language belongs to the Uralic language family?

(A) Libya
(B) Cambodia
(C) Kazakhstan
(D) Portugal
(E) Germany

124. Which of the following terms best describes the geographical boundary of one particular linguistic feature?

(A) Language border
(B) Toponym
(C) Choropleth interval
(D) Linguistic hearth
(E) Isogloss

125. Which of the following sacred places is most closely associated with animism?

(A) Hagia Sophia
(B) Ayers Rock
(C) Sistine Chapel
(D) Mecca
(E) The Western Wall

126. Historically, cultural diffusion patterns in the United States have tended to flow in which general direction?

(A) East to west
(B) West to east
(C) North to south
(D) South to north
(E) Northwest to southeast

127. A Hindu temple located in Texas is most likely the result of which kind of diffusion?

(A) Expansion
(B) Hierarchical
(C) Contagious
(D) Relocation
(E) Stimulus

128. The religious doctrine of *ahimsa*, which discourages violence against other living beings, is best associated with which of the following regions?

(A) North Africa
(B) Western Europe
(C) Arabian Peninsula
(D) Andes Mountains
(E) Indian Subcontinent

129. The persistence of ethnic urban enclaves in major American cities could be cited as evidence to support all of the following phenomena EXCEPT

(A) chain migration
(B) residential segregation
(C) structural assimilation
(D) multiculturalism
(E) multinucleated urban structure

130. Which of the following folk architecture styles is ideally suited for a diurnal climate, with high daytime temperatures and much lower evening temperatures?

(A) New York Dutch house
(B) Iroquois longhouse
(C) Garrison house
(D) Adobe house
(E) Log cabin

131. Compared to popular cultures, folk cultures are
    (A) more cosmopolitan
    (B) more homogeneous
    (C) more diffuse
    (D) more transitory
    (E) more contagious

132. A dialect is best classified as which of the following?
    (A) Cultural complex
    (B) Cultural trait
    (C) Language branch
    (D) Language group
    (E) Language family

133. A Mormon church located in a rural area of northwestern Colorado is most likely the result of which kind of diffusion?
    (A) Expansion
    (B) Relocation
    (C) Hierarchical
    (D) Maladaptive
    (E) Stimulus

134. Which of the following provides the clearest example of a derelict landscape?
    (A) A gentrified, urban landscape
    (B) A rural, cultivated landscape
    (C) A suburban, residential landscape
    (D) An abandoned, industrial landscape
    (E) A preserved, sacred landscape

135. The deliberate killing of a large group of people, especially those of a particular ethnic group, is called
    (A) a refugee crisis
    (B) infanticide
    (C) patricide
    (D) civilian casualties
    (E) genocide

136. In the core-domain-sphere model of cultural influence, what is the core?

(A) An area where a particular culture is dominant but not universal

(B) The area with the highest concentration of the culture

(C) An outlying zone where members of the culture may be a minority

(D) The urban city at the middle of a metropolitan region

(E) The center for economic activity in a country

137. A new fashion trend originating in New York City that diffuses to Los Angeles, Paris, and Tokyo before reaching rural areas of New York state would be an example of which of the following kinds of diffusion?

(A) Contagious

(B) Hierarchical

(C) Uniform

(D) Relocation

(E) Stimulus

138. The Sunbelt and New England are two examples of which kind of culture region?

(A) Functional

(B) Formal

(C) Vernacular

(D) Municipal

(E) Transnational

139. An immigrant who selectively adopts certain customs of the dominant host society in order to advance socioeconomically, while still retaining much of his or her native customs, practices, and beliefs, best illustrates the concept of

(A) acculturation

(B) maladaptive behavior

(C) assimilation

(D) ethnocentrism

(E) all of the above

140. A highly simplified language developed between linguistically heterogeneous groups for the purposes of basic intergroup communication is known as which of the following?

(A) Creole
(B) Pidgin
(C) Lingua franca
(D) Bilingualism
(E) Standard dialect

141. All of the following belong to the Indo-European language family EXCEPT

(A) Hindi
(B) Bengali
(C) Farsi
(D) Mandarin
(E) Dutch

142. A *minaret* is an architectural feature common to places of worship in which of the following religions?

(A) Buddhism
(B) Hinduism
(C) Christianity
(D) Judaism
(E) Islam

143. Which of the following toponyms best belongs in a formal culture region defined by common traits of Catholicism and Spanish language?

(A) Dar es Salaam
(B) Saint Paul
(C) San Jose
(D) Tel Aviv
(E) Fauske

144. Which of the following regions is characterized as a zone of conflict between Muslim and Hindu ethnic groups?

(A) Kurdistan
(B) Chechnya
(C) Kashmir
(D) East Timor
(E) The West Bank

145. All of the following are examples of iconic, secular landscapes EXCEPT

(A) the Eiffel Tower

(B) Mount Rushmore

(C) the Lincoln Memorial

(D) the Great Wall of China

(E) the Dome of the Rock

146. Lesotho, an independent state whose territorial borders are entirely surrounded by the Republic of South Africa, is an example of a(n)

(A) urban ghetto

(B) exclave

(C) city-state

(D) enclave

(E) province

147. Which of the following religions is most closely associated with proselytism?

(A) Hinduism

(B) Christianity

(C) Sikhism

(D) Islam

(E) Judaism

148. In which of the following countries are inhabitants subject to Sharia law?

(A) Saudi Arabia

(B) Venezuela

(C) Ethiopia

(D) Turkey

(E) North Korea

149. The predominance of English as the preferred language spoken at many international business meetings and political summits could be cited to support the claim that English is a popular

(A) Creole language

(B) pidgin language

(C) language branch

(D) dialect

(E) lingua franca

150. The Alhambra, a UNESCO World Heritage site located in southern Spain, is an elaborate palace that exhibits a blend of Islamic and Christian architectural influences. It was originally built by Muslim Moors in the 14th century, then later renovated by Catholic monarchs in the 16th century, following the reconquest of Spain. These cumulative influences evident throughout its landscape illustrate the concept of

   (A) stimulus diffusion
   (B) sequent occupance
   (C) environmental determinism
   (D) transhumance
   (E) distance decay

151. Telecommunication networks, whose areas of service radiate outward from central hubs, or nodes, best represent which of the following types of culture region?

   (A) Vernacular culture region
   (B) Formal culture region
   (C) Functional culture region
   (D) Folk culture region
   (E) Popular cultural region

152. A holistic approach to studying the relationship between a human society and its natural environment is known as

   (A) cultural ecology
   (B) environmental determinism
   (C) innovation adoption
   (D) topophilia
   (E) geomancy

153. A significant imbalance in the ratio of males to females in age cohorts under 30 in China, a result of the country's one-child policy, could be cited as evidence of all of the following EXCEPT

   (A) gender discrimination
   (B) authoritarian family planning
   (C) female infanticide
   (D) gender longevity gap
   (E) maladaptive behavior

154. The prohibition that forbids Hindus from slaughtering or consuming beef is an example of a(n)

(A) Sharia law
(B) religious proscription
(C) ethnic conflict
(D) animistic tradition
(E) secular belief

155. Which of the following religions did NOT originate in the Indian subcontinent?

(A) Buddhism
(B) Jainism
(C) Sikhism
(D) Hinduism
(E) Zoroastrianism

156. Two prominent French ethnic islands in North America are historically located in which of the following areas?

(A) Louisiana and Quebec
(B) Minnesota and Newfoundland
(C) New Brunswick and California
(D) Utah and Ontario
(E) Florida and Saskatchewan

157. The term *white flight* is associated with all of the following EXCEPT

(A) processes of suburban and exurban expansion
(B) the persistence of de facto racial segregation
(C) residential discriminatory practices, such as redlining
(D) processes of gentrification
(E) processes of economic restructuring and urban decay

158. Zionism is best defined as the

(A) Shinto ritual of purification involving ceremonial offerings and prayers
(B) Islamic custom of pilgrimage to Mecca that must be undertaken at least once during every follower's lifetime
(C) Mormon rite of passage that involves a two-year mission of service
(D) Confucian doctrine that urges respect for one's elders
(E) Jewish claim to Palestine as their rightful national homeland

159. Arabic, which spread westward with the diffusion of Islam, is part of which of the following language families?

(A) Sino-Tibetan
(B) Afro-Asiatic
(C) Indo-European
(D) Malayo-Polynesian
(E) Niger-Congo

160. The term *taboo* refers to

(A) body art and other body modifications
(B) a restriction on behavior based on local law
(C) a restriction on behavior based on social custom
(D) a common practice among people of a particular culture
(E) a generalization about people of a certain culture

161. Judaism, a religion based on the belief in one God, is best characterized as a

(A) syncretic religion
(B) monotheistic religion
(C) shamanistic religion
(D) proselytical religion
(E) secular religion

162. The belief in the inherent superiority of one's own culture is known as

(A) anthropocentrism
(B) ethnography
(C) acculturation
(D) ethnocentrism
(E) assimilation

163. Which of the following is a sacred place in the Hindu religion?

(A) Dead Sea
(B) Ganges River
(C) Mount Fuji
(D) Sahara Desert
(E) Tierra del Fuego

164. All of the following are traits common to Muslim regions of the world EXCEPT

(A) fasting
(B) pilgrimage
(C) Sharia law
(D) polytheism
(E) daily ritual prayers

165. All of the following are true of language isolates like Basque and Ainu EXCEPT

(A) They have no demonstrable connection to other known existing world languages.
(B) Constructed languages like Esperanto also fit within the definition of a language isolate.
(C) They often exist in geographically isolated areas, but not exclusively.
(D) Many language isolates are in danger of extinction due to declining numbers of native speakers.
(E) Korean, for which no connection to other Sino-Tibetan languages has been proven, is considered the most widely spoken language isolate.

166. A reconstructed language from which a number of related, modern languages all derive is known as a(n)

(A) protolanguage
(B) artifact
(C) Creole language
(D) standard dialect
(E) pidgin language

167. The English language belongs to which of the following branches of the Indo-European language family?

(A) Romanic
(B) Hellenic
(C) Celtic
(D) Germanic
(E) Armenian

168. In Islam the religious practice of "sacred struggle" is known as

(A) hajj
(B) Ramadan
(C) jihad
(D) Shabbat
(E) brahmacharya

169. The concept of nirvana is most closely associated with which of the following religions?

(A) Confucianism
(B) Islam
(C) Animism
(D) Judaism
(E) Buddhism

170. In which of the following countries is one most likely to encounter speakers whose native tongue belongs to the Nilo-Saharan language family?

(A) Chad
(B) Kuwait
(C) Turkey
(D) Mongolia
(E) Cyprus

171. Which of the following Amerindian languages corresponds to the Yucatan Peninsula of Mexico?

(A) Comanche
(B) Algonquin
(C) Mayan
(D) Cherokee
(E) Lakota

172. A collection of languages related to each other through a common ancestor language that existed before recorded human history is called a

(A) language family
(B) kinship group
(C) folk culture
(D) speech community
(E) language group

173. Which of the following countries was the site of violent religious conflicts between Catholic and Protestant Christian groups throughout much of the 20th century?

(A) Costa Rica
(B) Canada
(C) Ireland
(D) Switzerland
(E) Greece

174. A social decline in religious adherence is referred to as

(A) partisanship
(B) fundamentalism
(C) syncretism
(D) mysticism
(E) secularism

175. Which of the following culture regions of the United States has the strongest historical connections to Lutheran Christian traditions?

(A) The Rocky Mountains
(B) New England
(C) The Upper Midwest
(D) The South
(E) The Pacific Northwest

176. The term *caste* refers to a particular system of social stratification that is informed by which of the following religions?

(A) Buddhism
(B) Hinduism
(C) Confucianism
(D) Taoism
(E) Islam

177. Shinto, a set of rituals and customs that are practiced in order to connect with ancient spirits, is a religious tradition that belongs to which of the following nations?

(A) Japan
(B) China
(C) Nepal
(D) Bolivia
(E) Tibet

178. Which of the following areas describes a conflict region between various ethnic groups, including Serbs, Albanians, and Bosnians?

   (A) The Persian Gulf
   (B) The West Bank
   (C) The Himalayans
   (D) The Balkan Peninsula
   (E) The Horn of Africa

179. The largest branch of Islam, to which as many as 80 percent of all Muslims belong, is called

   (A) Dravidian
   (B) Shia
   (C) Meccan
   (D) Berber
   (E) Sunni

180. The contrast between different groups of society that is based on cultural issues, such as race, class, or sexuality, NOT location, is called

   (A) social dialect
   (B) colonialism
   (C) ethnic cleansing
   (D) social distance
   (E) cultural nationalism

181. A small religious group that is an offshoot of a larger established religion is called a

   (A) church
   (B) cult
   (C) denomination
   (D) sect
   (E) quorum

182. All of the following are examples of material culture in North America EXCEPT

   (A) angled-rail or snake fences
   (B) mound houses
   (C) Quebec cabins
   (D) Amish horse carriages
   (E) bluegrass gospel songs

183. The Norman cottage is a distinct style of vernacular architecture that was introduced to North America through relocation diffusion and that is modeled after an architectural style native to the Normandy region of France. Given this information, which of the following regions of North America is most likely to feature the Norman cottage?

   (A) Montana
   (B) Sonora
   (C) Arkansas
   (D) Quebec
   (E) West Virginia

184. Which of the following U.S. cities best belongs in a vernacular culture region known as the Corn Belt?

   (A) Bangor, ME
   (B) Chattanooga, TN
   (C) Lincoln, NE
   (D) Raleigh, NC
   (E) Provo, UT

185. The toponyms *Leninskoye* and *Stalinsk* are most likely to be found in which of the following countries?

   (A) Russia
   (B) Armenia
   (C) Cuba
   (D) Uzbekistan
   (E) Malaysia

186. Which of the following terms refers to a language that experienced near extinction but now has an increasing number of speakers, often due to a deliberate educational effort?

   (A) A dead language
   (B) An Indo-European language
   (C) A revived language
   (D) A suppressed language
   (E) A regional dialect

187. Which of these terms best describes a religion that is passed from generation to generation in one specific culture and rarely seeks out new members or converts?

(A) Ethnic religion
(B) Universalizing religion
(C) Hierarchical religion
(D) Monotheistic religion
(E) Autonomous religion

188. The country of Papua New Guinea boasts one of the world's highest rates of linguistic diversity, with more than 800 documented indigenous languages. This linguistic diversity has been preserved largely because of the country's rugged geography, which includes mountains and islands that have tended to keep different speech communities isolated from one another. In the context of Papua New Guinea's geography of language, mountains and islands represent

(A) intervening opportunities
(B) language paths
(C) critical distances
(D) barriers to diffusion
(E) cultural innovations

189. The place or area where a cultural practice originates is known as a(n)

(A) cosmos
(B) frontier
(C) edge
(D) path
(E) hearth

190. The two largest language families in the world, in terms of absolute numbers of speakers, are

(A) Afro-Asiatic and Austro-Asiatic
(B) Japanese-Korean and Niger-Congo
(C) Sino-Tibetan and Indo-European
(D) Amerindian and Malayo-Polynesian
(E) Uralic-Altaic and Australian

191. An urban ethnic enclave that is held together by external forces of discrimination and marginalization, as well as by internal forces of community identity and ethnic solidarity, is known as a(n)

(A) exclave
(B) ghetto
(C) gated community
(D) commune
(E) isogloss

192. Which of the following terms refers to one culture's dominance over another culture, often as a result of forceful control?

(A) Assimilation
(B) Cultural imperialism
(C) Acculturation
(D) Gerrymandering
(E) Cultural autonomy

193. The following figure is a cognitive map created by "Sandra," a 10-year-old girl who lives in a suburban community in the United States.

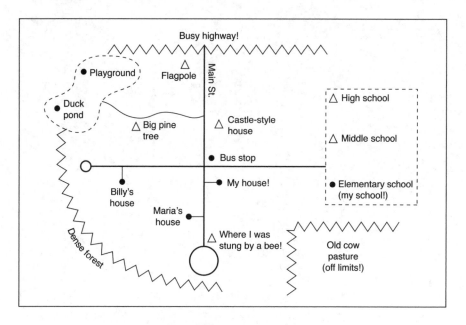

(A) Briefly define the five standard elements of cognitive mapping: path, district, edge, node, and landmark. Cite a few examples for each element to illustrate your explanation.

(B) Describe how each of these five elements is thematically represented in Sandra's mental map.

(C) Briefly explain two major ways that cognitive maps differ from more objective cartographic representations of space.

194. The idea that the earth's surface can be territorially divided into different cultural regions offers an effective approach for organizing space in human geography. Yet despite the effectiveness of the cultural region approach, there is clearly no one right way to organize geographies of culture into distinct regions.

(A) Define the three major kinds of cultural regions studied in human geography: formal, functional, and vernacular. Provide at least one example for each definition.

(B) Briefly explain one advantage and one drawback to organizing space according to each of these cultural region approaches.

CHAPTER 4

The Political Organization of Space

195. Many borders act to create cultural distance between people of the same ethnic group, a phenomenon that most often leads to

(A) the militarization of that ethnic group
(B) the fragmentation of that ethnic group
(C) the unification of that ethnic group
(D) the blending of that ethnic group with at least two other ethnic groups
(E) the political rise of that ethnic group

196. Transnational migrants and immigrants maintain human networks primarily by

(A) remaining in contact with persons from their state of origin
(B) petitioning federal governments to prohibit human trafficking
(C) failing to adopt the customs of their new homeland
(D) establishing small businesses in urban areas
(E) becoming citizens of their new homelands within a few years after becoming expatriates

197. The presence of a national boundary between two cities has the potential to decrease the amount of trade that occurs between them if

(A) the two countries in which the cities are located have tariffs on certain goods
(B) the two countries in which the cities are located are party to a free trade agreement
(C) the two countries in which the cities are located do not share a common port
(D) the two countries in which the cities are located are both clients of the World Bank
(E) the two countries in which the cities are located are connected by expressways

198. Cities along national borders often contain evidence of the interdependence that exists between two states, which is demonstrated on an individual level by residents of these cities who

(A) frequently tell stories about the two states
(B) frequently migrate between the two states
(C) frequently pass legislation regarding the two states
(D) frequently work only in one state
(E) frequently are tourists in a third state

199. Some states, such as India and Nepal, have treaties that allow citizens to live, work, and travel freely in both lands, a practice that typically leads to the development of

(A) opposing national identities
(B) fluid national identities
(C) rigid national identities
(D) postindustrial national identities
(E) Communist national identities

200. A federal state is likely to possess

(A) citizens who favor democratic elections
(B) a leader with the power to revise the state's constitution
(C) a large amount of mineral resources
(D) multiple systems of checks and balances
(E) a king and queen

201. A state that is governed by a single centralized power with little power given to subnational units except as deemed by the central government is called a

(A) puppet state
(B) Communist state
(C) federal state
(D) single-party state
(E) unitary state

202. A confederacy or union between territories, regions, or other entities is most likely to arise in a

(A) federal state
(B) unitary state
(C) puppet state
(D) monarchy
(E) Communist state

203. The centralized power of a unitary state is most likely to be threatened by the development of

(A) a self-governing region
(B) a broad trade agreement with a neighboring state
(C) a constitution that requires citizens to be born within the state
(D) voting districts that divide large rural areas
(E) a new religion found only within the state

204. When several unitary states choose to become one state, their initial attempt to govern themselves is likely to take the form of a

(A) series of colonizations
(B) series of civil wars
(C) series of annexations of territory
(D) series of treaties
(E) series of redistricting efforts

205. Most of the world's unitary states can be found on the continents of

(A) North America and South America
(B) Africa and Asia
(C) Australia and Europe
(D) Antarctica and North America
(E) Australia and South America

206. A buffer state is a politically neutral state that lies between two more powerful states and acts

(A) to enhance both states' political powers
(B) as a taxing authority for both states
(C) to balance power between the two states
(D) to minimize the religious authority of major institutions
(E) to stop immigrants from traveling to the larger of the two states

207. Today, states act to establish control over disputed areas of the sea primarily by

(A) charting endangered species in uninhabited coastal areas

(B) attending international conventions on maritime law

(C) mapping uncharted areas of the world's oceans using advanced technology

(D) engaging in economic activities in coastal areas and open waters

(E) allocating funding to increase the size of their naval forces

208. Territoriality is the practice of creating geographic boundaries in response to social and political conditions and typically acts to

(A) separate different populations by culture

(B) reaffirm ethnic ties between different populations

(C) stop the sharing of languages and religions between two neighboring ethnic groups

(D) link the economies of two neighboring states

(E) strengthen trade relations between wealthy and less wealthy states

209. People divide a continent into regional trade blocs primarily to

(A) increase the amount of fair trade

(B) promote the goal of global free trade

(C) strengthen economic ties between member states

(D) form cultural links between former military enemies

(E) weaken the influence of communism

210. A boundary that was put in place by an outside, conquering, or other political power that ignores the cultural organizations of the landscape is called a

(A) cultural boundary

(B) physical boundary

(C) relic boundary

(D) superimposed boundary

(E) buffer state

211. The geographic boundary of a state can also be a physical boundary, such as a

(A) religious movement
(B) lake or mountain
(C) language barrier
(D) type of currency
(E) national dish

212. One example of a geometric political boundary is the

(A) cultural divide between Creole and Cajun communities in New Orleans, Louisiana
(B) straight line of the George Washington Bridge between New York and New Jersey
(C) sharp ascent of the Sierra Nevada
(D) curve of Ohio's coast around Lake Erie
(E) straight line between the states of Colorado and Kansas

213. Political boundaries existed in the ancient world and were often maintained by small groups at

(A) agricultural storehouses
(B) defensive fortresses
(C) scientific research stations
(D) open-air marketplaces
(E) seasonal hunting camps

214. In democratic nations, legislators and political parties typically redraw boundaries for voting districts after the release of data from a

(A) national geographical survey
(B) state public opinion poll
(C) state primary election
(D) national census
(E) national study on spending patterns

215. A conflict over the sharing of the water in the Kaveri River between the south Indian states of Karnataka and Tamil Nadu would best be classified as a(n)

(A) allocational boundary dispute
(B) locational boundary dispute
(C) operational boundary dispute
(D) definitional boundary dispute
(E) genetic boundary dispute

216. A separation fence, such as that which exists on the territory between India and Pakistan, is most often used to demarcate a(n)

(A) cease-fire line
(B) cross-border region
(C) linguistic border
(D) annexed zone
(E) decolonized territory

217. During the 20th century, the collapse of intricate political networks, such as existed in the Union of Soviet Socialist Republics (USSR), led to the understanding that

(A) strong economic ties are necessary to overcome major ethnic differences
(B) trade partners should not work together to develop alternative energy sources
(C) nations should eliminate their trade tariffs to encourage economic security
(D) environmental justice campaigns fail to adequately identify the hardest-hit areas
(E) politicians must implement global, rather than local, antiterrorist policies

218. When a nation-state undergoes a revolution, there is a high likelihood that its citizens will leave, causing an

(A) increase in trade tariffs in neighboring states
(B) increase in the mechanization of labor in neighboring states
(C) increase in environmental equity in neighboring states
(D) increase in ethnic diversity in neighboring states
(E) increase in economic stability in neighboring states

219. The practice termed *environmental racism* involves a majority population using political representation to

(A) request funding for alternative energy sources

(B) remove toxic waste to sites that are far from its residential communities and businesses and often located near minority populations

(C) demand that public parks and natural preserves be segregated

(D) require cleanup efforts to take place in minority communities

(E) propose legislation that does not adversely affect minority communities

220. A state that contains many environmental zones, such as coast, mountains, and desert, is likely to have residents who are

(A) opposed to modernization and technology

(B) politically active

(C) members of religions that are also found in neighboring states

(D) ethnically similar

(E) socially and politically separate

221. When two states begin to compete with one another economically, they are most likely to become

(A) trade partners

(B) politically unstable

(C) political antagonists

(D) multicultural democracies

(E) colonies of large empires

222. A nation-state is most often defined by its twin attributes of sovereignty and

(A) religious tolerance

(B) social democracy

(C) ethnic homogeneity

(D) economic prosperity

(E) a strong antiterrorist policy

223. The Exclusive Economic Zone (EEZ), established by the United Nations, refers to

    (A) the creation of the European Union (EU)
    (B) the part of the ocean a coastal state has exclusive mineral and fishing rights over
    (C) a group of developing countries that require foreign aid
    (D) the North American Free Trade Agreement creating a trilateral trade block in North America
    (E) zones within a state where the trade laws are different than the rest of the state

224. A political leader might seek to make his or her state conform to the traditional concept of a nation-state by

    (A) demanding representation in the United Nations
    (B) openly encouraging civil disobedience
    (C) instituting a bicameral system of legislature
    (D) using the popular media to promote the idea of a national culture
    (E) advocating a policy of multiculturalism

225. The government's role in the development of a nation-state is critical because the government is required to

    (A) protect its borders and resolve any internal conflicts
    (B) locate and restore lost items of cultural heritage
    (C) serve as an intermediary to resolve conflicts between its religious leaders
    (D) prevent the exportation of local agricultural products
    (E) take part in international talks regarding economic globalization

226. Which of the following events has the most potential to determine whether a nation will remain a nation-state?

    (A) A rejection of capitalism
    (B) A reduction in the availability of mineral resources
    (C) A large influx of immigrants
    (D) A development of a national scientific research program
    (E) A sudden natural disaster

227. The leader of a nation-state would be likely to reject an intergovernmental action that

(A) recognized a cultural monument important to the primary ethnic group of the state

(B) formed the foundation of a peace agreement

(C) promoted the concept of self-governance

(D) added protections for existing maritime borders

(E) required land to be swapped between itself and another country

228. Gerrymandering is a practice in which a political party attempts to gain an unequal advantage by

(A) nominating a candidate who challenges the state's constitution

(B) advocating that the electoral college be replaced by the popular vote

(C) changing the boundaries of a legislative district

(D) electing a party chairperson who is a friend of the current president

(E) seeking the support of labor unions

229. The Arab League, an international organization of Arab states, limits the sovereign power of its members by

(A) planning joint attacks on common enemies

(B) promoting tourism in member states

(C) coordinating free trade agreements among member states

(D) funding the building of wells in member states

(E) failing to count the number of literate citizens in member states

230. The fragmentation of the Roman Empire that occurred between the first and third centuries BCE most likely led to the

(A) acquisition of new territories by the empire

(B) destabilization of the empire's outer frontiers

(C) homogenization of the empire's largest cities

(D) abolishment of slavery in regions beyond the empire

(E) development of agricultural lands within the empire's smaller cities

231. When a sovereign state undergoes the political process of devolution, it grants some of the powers of

(A) its local governments to its state governments

(B) its central government to the government of another sovereign state

(C) its local governments to its central government

(D) its central government to its regional governments

(E) its colonies to its central government

232. Both domestic and international acts of terror are defined as terrorism because both

(A) have the effect of intimidating a group of people through violence

(B) can be perpetrated by groups that believe in civil disobedience

(C) have been outlawed by antiterrorist legislation

(D) can be traced to radical religious doctrines

(E) are organized through digital communication such as e-mail

233. The study of electoral geography is best conducted in

(A) democratic states

(B) Communist states

(C) dictatorships

(D) monarchies

(E) territories and colonies

234. One of the most notable acts to limit a state's sovereignty took place after World War II, when some of the states that had made up the Allied forces

(A) awarded political asylum to German citizens who had cared for war orphans

(B) elected a prime minister for Germany

(C) used Germany's ports for commercial ventures

(D) conducted a series of military tribunals in Germany

(E) destroyed Germany's capital city

235. The North Atlantic Treaty Organization (NATO) is one of the world's most powerful

(A) atomic energy commissions
(B) military alliances
(C) trade organizations
(D) fiscal unions
(E) cultural heritage councils

236. One of the classic examples of supranationalism is the European Union (EU) because this body of member states has

(A) transferred some of its powers to a central authority
(B) invested all of its power in a prime minister
(C) a single annual election
(D) a single intergovernmental bank
(E) required its member states not to sign international treaties

237. Which of the following events could be mapped using geographic mapping techniques to illustrate how terrorism affects communities?

(A) The stages of antiterrorist legislation before it is passed into law
(B) The stories of how would-be terrorists were convinced not to carry out suicide attacks
(C) The migration of survivors of an urban bombing attack to an empty rural area
(D) A technical description of how improvised explosive devices (IEDs) work
(E) A determination of which of two cities will rebuild after a civil war

238. Electoral geographers study

(A) the interactions between place and how people vote
(B) the interaction between place and how people migrate
(C) the ethnicity of different populations within certain areas
(D) how media coverage influences elections
(E) the history of geography

239. The United Nations has a policy of using economic and military sanctions to limit the sovereign powers of

(A) only contested states

(B) humanitarian organizations such as the Red Cross

(C) any state that disrupts international peace

(D) only its member states

(E) territories of nonmember states

240. Australia is a union rather than an alliance because its states are governed by

(A) a United Nations security force

(B) a common constitution

(C) common police forces

(D) the British Parliament

(E) members of two opposing political parties

241. Large states such as Canada have used devolution to allow populations in distant, resource-rich areas to

(A) gain representation in the national parliament in exchange for a share of the resources

(B) engage in more self-government in exchange for a share of the resources

(C) determine international borders for their areas in exchange for a share of the resources

(D) select the official language of the nation in exchange for a share of the resources

(E) participate in global economic forums in exchange for a share of the resources

242. When an act of terrorism occurs within a democratic state, a common response by the national government is to

(A) limit the powers of the president or prime minister

(B) limit the number of children a couple is allowed to have

(C) limit the number of individuals who receive government grants

(D) limit the civil liberties of citizens and noncitizens

(E) limit the funding of agencies that police criminal activity

243. Political cleavages, significant differences that determine how individuals will cast their vote in an election, typically

(A) are found only in former dictatorships

(B) have primarily been studied in Asian states

(C) vary widely, ranging from religion to place of residence

(D) are linked only to economic class

(E) cannot be found in states that were previously Communist states

244. Nongovernmental organizations (NGOs) often motivate the global community to limit the sovereign powers of states by publicizing data indicating that the states

(A) refused to participate in the global economy

(B) violated the human rights of their citizens

(C) failed to provide refugees with legal counselors

(D) have not created national constitutions

(E) have not developed any environmental policies

245. Before the 1960s, India's caste system was a powerful social force, and partly explained the state's

(A) extreme political fragmentation

(B) identity as a secular nation

(C) continued political alliance with China

(D) unification after the end of British rule

(E) fight not to be conquered by Muslim rulers

246. A supranational resolution is one that is signed by a

(A) group of powerful states within a nation

(B) group of different nations

(C) group of territories that belong to a nation

(D) group of counties within a state

(E) group of businesses within a nation

247. In the New World, some colonists used religion to convert indigenous groups with the aim of

(A) developing indigenous groups' rights to mineral resources

(B) allowing indigenous groups to fight for access to deep forests

(C) helping indigenous groups to develop new technologies

(D) encouraging indigenous groups to practice forms of traditional medicine

(E) creating a more hospitable environment to further colonization

248. Spain colonized much of Central and South America, yet in the 19th century, the end result of these efforts was

(A) a war between Spain and its territories in North Africa

(B) a war between Central America and the largest nations in South America

(C) a series of government strikes in Spain and Portugal

(D) a series of revolutionary movements in Central and South America

(E) the unification of Spain's Central American and South American colonies

249. Between the 15th and 19th centuries, a multitude of European nations engaged in imperialism in India primarily by

(A) requiring all citizens to convert to Islam

(B) developing computer technology and the Internet

(C) instituting a group of chartered trading companies

(D) engaging in a series of intense air battles with Indian forces

(E) educating African immigrants in India

250. Which group of people tends to link the people of a colonizing state and the people of a colony?

(A) A tribe indigenous to the colony

(B) A hired foreign military force

(C) Settlers from the colonizing state

(D) Slaves from a third state

(E) Diplomats of an international organization

251. Between the 18th and 20th centuries, the national governments of the United States and Canada employed an imperialist policy of developing land for new immigrants and

(A) removing indigenous groups to reservations

(B) granting indigenous groups the right to tax national governments

(C) mandating that indigenous groups protect monuments of cultural heritage

(D) requiring indigenous groups to build national railroads

(E) providing indigenous groups with firepower

252. Western imperialist policies of the 20th and 21st centuries have been most deeply influenced by

(A) South African imperialism
(B) Belgian imperialism
(C) German imperialism
(D) Portuguese imperialism
(E) British imperialism

253. A state undergoing the transition from a dictatorship to a democracy must provide its citizens with

(A) monetary reparations
(B) water rights
(C) civil liberties
(D) firepower
(E) diplomatic immunity

254. Participatory democracy in the United States increased in the years immediately after the Civil War due to the

(A) development of voting rights for African Americans
(B) development of property rights for African Americans
(C) development of property rights for Asian Americans
(D) development of voting rights for women
(E) development of property rights for women

255. In 1983, after years of political instability, Argentina reinstituted a democratic government, indicating that

(A) elections must be monitored by the international community to establish a democracy
(B) elections must be conducted by the government in power to establish a democracy
(C) elections must be free and open to the majority of the population to establish a democracy
(D) elections must be conducted by governments of other nations to establish a democracy
(E) elections must be held on an annual basis to establish a democracy

256. Some geographers argue that a nation in political turmoil can become a democracy more quickly if foreign governments use their military power to influence the nation's affairs. They often cite as a primary example

(A) China following the Boxer Rebellion
(B) Germany following World War II
(C) Ireland following the Troubles
(D) Pakistan following the partition of India
(E) Haiti following World War I

257. Democratization can be a slow process, with a common step between the acceptance of an authoritarian government and the election of a president or prime minister being the

(A) colonization of an island nation
(B) recognition of a divine monarchy
(C) elimination of the judicial branch
(D) establishment of a legislative body
(E) transition to an information-based economy

258. Since the former Union of Soviet Socialist Republics (USSR) collapsed, the majority of smaller states that formerly made up the USSR have

(A) completely eliminated their sovereign powers
(B) assigned their sovereign powers to other states
(C) strengthened their sovereign powers
(D) reduced their number of sovereign powers
(E) failed to develop any sovereign powers

259. An agreement between two neighboring governments that would grant many members of a certain ethnic group citizenship to both states would be likely to lead to

(A) unification of this ethnic community
(B) fragmentation of this ethnic community
(C) assimilation of this ethnic community
(D) dispersal of this ethnic community
(E) destruction of this ethnic community

260. Basque groups could directly force a devolution of the Spanish government by
    (A) forming an alliance with Basque groups in other nations
    (B) gaining political control over certain areas of Spain
    (C) participating in a global economic forum
    (D) electing a Basque president
    (E) voicing their political concerns in a meeting of Spain's Senate

261. The lack of political unity among nations in the Middle East makes it difficult for these states to
    (A) form any economic alliances
    (B) attend meetings of the United Nations Security Council
    (C) participate in global environmental forums
    (D) develop their respective urban areas
    (E) address supranational issues in the region

262. The formation of a federation, particularly one in which two previously separate states put aside their political differences, involves an act of
    (A) exile
    (B) defense
    (C) opposition
    (D) unification
    (E) comparison

263. When a nation possesses a resource that its neighbors desire, the neighboring nations are likely try to gain control of the resource by
    (A) assisting the nation in question in developing more sovereign powers
    (B) advocating that no nation in the region possess sovereign powers
    (C) limiting the nation in question from utilizing its existing sovereign powers
    (D) participating in a global council to determine the nature of sovereign powers
    (E) educating their citizens about the importance of sovereign powers

264. The end of the Cold War provided electoral geographers with the first opportunity to study modern political cleavages in

(A) Canada and Australia
(B) Poland and the Czech Republic
(C) the United States and Mexico
(D) France and the United Kingdom
(E) Jamaica and Bermuda

265. Use the following maps of Louisiana's old and new congressional districts to answer the questions below.

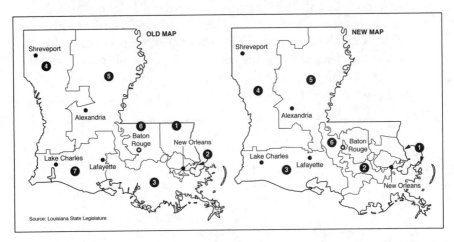

Source: Louisiana State Legislature

(A) The 2011 action to redistrict Louisiana has created six new congressional districts. Determine why Louisiana now has six instead of seven seats in the United States House of Representatives. Describe how the change may affect citizens of the state.

(B) Louisiana's second congressional district, based in New Orleans, is the only district in the state in which the majority of the citizens are African American. This district was extended west to Baton Rouge to include more African American voters. Identify an additional reason this district was extended. Also, describe the result of including more territory in the second district.

(C) Louisiana's 2011 redistricting action was required to be approved by the Louisiana Legislature. Then it was required to be approved by the United States Department of Justice to make sure it was in accord with the Voting Rights Act. Describe three other methods that the U.S. government uses to protect African Americans' right to vote, thereby affecting electoral geography.

266. Northern Ireland is one of the four states that make up the United
Kingdom, together with England, Scotland, and Wales. Between
the late 1960s and 1998, a group of Northern Ireland nationalists
used terrorist attacks to demand that Northern Ireland become part
of the Republic of Ireland. These nationalists perpetrated violent
acts in Northern Ireland, England, the Republic of Ireland, and the
European mainland. Use this information and the following two
maps to answer the questions below.

(A) Describe three methods that the states of the United Kingdom could have used to protect themselves from terrorist attacks.

(B) Explain how Northern Ireland's geographic and cultural proximity to the European mainland made other European states a possible target for terrorist attacks.

(C) In 1998, the two opposing sides in the conflict signed the Belfast Agreement. This agreement led to Northern Ireland becoming more self-governing. How has the devolution helped to reduce the number of terrorist attacks within the state?

CHAPTER 5

Agriculture and Rural Land Use

267. The Second Agricultural Revolution occurred at roughly the same time as the

(A) American Civil War
(B) Industrial Revolution
(C) Green Revolution
(D) Boxer Rebellion
(E) California Gold Rush

268. The Third Agricultural Revolution is also known as the

(A) Green Revolution
(B) Industrial Revolution
(C) Genetic Revolution
(D) Rice Revolution
(E) Plantation Revolution

269. Locations farthest from large bodies of water

(A) experience the most natural disasters
(B) have the most extreme climates
(C) are most suitable for large-scale agriculture
(D) need more water to irrigate crops
(E) tend to have the highest population density

270. Dogs, pigs, and chickens were first domesticated in

(A) Western Africa
(B) Central America
(C) North America
(D) Southeast Asia
(E) Northern India

271. All of the following are forms of commercial agriculture EXCEPT

(A) dairy farming
(B) specialized fruit production
(C) cattle ranching
(D) grain farming
(E) pastoral nomadism

272. A farmer plants corn in a field one year, cotton in the same field the following year, and then corn again. This farmer is practicing

(A) subsistence agriculture
(B) commercial farming
(C) crop rotation
(D) slash-and-burn agriculture
(E) shifting cultivation

273. Which of the following crops is grown on the sides of terraced hills to allow irrigation of the plants?

(A) Wheat
(B) Rice
(C) Taro
(D) Soybeans
(E) Millet

274. Which of the following seed crops were first domesticated in Mexico?

(A) Rice and wheat
(B) Corn and millet
(C) Yams and palm trees
(D) Squash and beans
(E) Sugarcane and taro

275. In South America, most ethanol is produced using

(A) corn
(B) soybeans
(C) wheat
(D) palm oil
(E) sugarcane

276. Market-gardening activities occur in which zone of von Thünen's model of agricultural land use?

(A) First zone
(B) Second zone
(C) Third zone
(D) Fourth zone
(E) Sixth zone

277. Which of the following was a short-term result of the collectivization of agricultural production in Communist states?

(A) Increased labor costs
(B) Urbanization
(C) Deindustrialization
(D) Food shortages
(E) Lower food costs

278. All of the following are plantation crops EXCEPT

(A) cotton
(B) tea
(C) sugarcane
(D) rubber
(E) wheat

279. Cash-cropping is a form of

(A) subsistence agriculture
(B) extensive agriculture
(C) pastoral nomadism
(D) mixed farming
(E) aquaculture

280. Which of the following methods of farming has become more popular in response to the widespread use of pesticides in farming?

(A) Slash-and-burn agriculture
(B) Crop rotation
(C) Organic farming
(D) Shifting cultivation
(E) Agricultural industrialization

281. All of the following crops might be grown on a truck farm EXCEPT

(A) green beans
(B) okra
(C) strawberries
(D) watermelons
(E) rice

282. The emergence of which of the following allowed people to settle in one location permanently rather than migrating seasonally?

(A) Subsistence farming
(B) Multicropping
(C) Monoculture
(D) Plantation agriculture
(E) Commercial farming

283. Which of the following was developed during the Third Agricultural Revolution?

(A) The cotton gin
(B) Animal domestication
(C) Cattle ranching
(D) Higher-yield hybrid plants
(E) Seed agriculture

284. Which of the following crops was domesticated in northern Africa approximately 1,200 years ago?

(A) Pineapples
(B) Coffee
(C) Squash
(D) Corn
(E) Millet

285. When flying across the central United States, the view consists of patches of land about one square mile in size. This is evidence of which type of land-use pattern?

(A) Metes and bounds system
(B) Long lots system
(C) Township and range system
(D) Sectional system
(E) Homestead system

286. Which of the following is true about agriculture in China?

(A) The government dictates the types and quantities of crops grown.

(B) China has the highest sanitary and phytosanitary standards in Asia.

(C) Both rice and wheat are grown throughout China.

(D) Organic farming accounts for most of the farming in China.

(E) China is the largest exporter of agricultural goods in the world.

287. Which of the following describes how winter wheat is planted and harvested?

(A) Planted in the fall, harvested in the winter

(B) Planted in the spring, harvested in the summer

(C) Planted in the winter, harvested in the spring

(D) Planted in the spring, harvested in the winter

(E) Planted in the fall, harvested in the summer or fall

288. Which of the following machines is used to cut grain that is standing in the fields?

(A) Tillage

(B) Reaper

(C) Thresher

(D) Harrow

(E) Transplanter

289. Decaying plant matter that can be converted into a source of alternative energy used to generate electricity or power engines can come from

(A) biodiversity

(B) solar power

(C) biomass

(D) organic conversion

(E) fermentation

290. A form of commercial agriculture that involves livestock grazing over a large area is called

(A) horticulture
(B) commercial gardening
(C) dairy farming
(D) pasturing
(E) ranching

291. When residents oppose a proposal for a new development or structure (such as a prison, a landfill, or a wind turbine) being built close to their homes or businesses, that is an example of

(A) NIMBYism
(B) topicide
(C) sustainable development
(D) desertification
(E) agribusiness

292. Farming on long lots is most likely to occur along which of the following?

(A) Mississippi River
(B) Salinas Valley
(C) Appalachian Mountains
(D) Great Plains
(E) Everglades

293. All of the following crops are products of Mediterranean agriculture EXCEPT

(A) olives
(B) grapes
(C) dates
(D) figs
(E) apples

294. Which of the following refers to the practice of growing just enough food to provide for one's own family?

(A) Subsistence agriculture
(B) Substitution principle
(C) Sustainable development
(D) Conservation
(E) Recycling

295. Which of the following describes an example of creative destruction?

(A) A farmer clears a forest in order to plant grain.

(B) A developer uses landfill to build a restaurant on a river.

(C) A farmer plants an orchard next to a field where cattle graze.

(D) A farmer plants corn in a field where grain was previously grown.

(E) A developer plants native plants around a shopping center.

296. Agriculture that requires a high level of manual effort is called

(A) reaping

(B) labor-intensive farming

(C) cultivation

(D) crop rotation

(E) preservation

297. Mineral fuels are also known as

(A) renewable resources

(B) coal

(C) fossil fuels

(D) stored reserves

(E) natural resources

298. In the preservationist land use model, people are encouraged to

(A) not alter the natural environment

(B) clear only land that is not currently in use

(C) raise only enough crops to feed the local population

(D) explore wilderness areas previously untouched

(E) raise only those crops that do not require irrigation

299. The process of taming animals to be comfortable around humans to provide necessary resources is called

(A) animal cruelty

(B) animal domestication

(C) ranching

(D) pasturing

(E) organic farming

300. The theory that people will do what is in their own best interest even when it is NOT in the best interest of the common good is called the

(A) theory of the common good
(B) theory of nonsustainability
(C) tragedy of the commons
(D) comedy of the anticommons
(E) theory of best self-interest

301. Herders who move herds constantly in order to find food sources as old sources are depleted engage in

(A) shifting cultivation
(B) pastoral nomadism
(C) commercial farming
(D) agropastoralism
(E) sedentarization

302. Which of the following is an example of the implementation of the sustainable land use model?

(A) A logger who cuts down trees for lumber plants more trees.
(B) A farmer plants a secondary crop in the space between the primary crops.
(C) A farmer plants only what is needed to feed his or her family.
(D) A herder moves from one location to another in order to find food for his or her herd.
(E) A developer clears a plot of land for a shopping mall and makes a donation to a conservation fund.

303. Which of the following types of agriculture is used most widely throughout the world?

(A) Commercial farming
(B) Slash-and-burn
(C) Plantation
(D) Shifting cultivation
(E) Mediterranean

304. Which form of commercial agriculture is found primarily in developing states?

(A) Plantation agriculture
(B) Livestock farming
(C) Mixed farming
(D) Dairy farming
(E) Truck farming

305. All of the following states are located in the Corn Belt EXCEPT

(A) Nebraska
(B) Illinois
(C) Indiana
(D) Montana
(E) Kansas

306. Which of the following crops is grown in the greatest quantity worldwide?

(A) Tobacco
(B) Cereal grains
(C) Sugarcane
(D) Potatoes
(E) Soybeans

307. Which of the following is an example of voluntary collective farming?

(A) Collectives in Vietnam between 1976 and 1986
(B) Cooperatives in Hungary between 1948 and 1956
(C) Collectives in Cuba between 1977 and 1983
(D) Kibbutzim in Israel between 1909 and the present
(E) Kolkhozy in the Soviet Union between 1928 and 1933

308. A type of animal feeding operation (AFO) that prepares an animal for slaughter by increasing the weight of the animal is called

(A) dairying
(B) a grazing farm
(C) a feedlot
(D) a cattle drive
(E) a livestock yard

309. Intertillage is the process of

(A) resting land between crop cycles
(B) planting between the rows of crops
(C) hand picking fruit yields
(D) transporting crops to market
(E) harvesting cereal crops with machinery

310. Which of the following is NOT an example of a staple food in Central America?

(A) Beans
(B) Wheat
(C) Corn
(D) Potatoes
(E) Squash

311. A society that relies on the cultivation of land is known as

(A) municipal
(B) metropolitan
(C) naturalist
(D) hunter-gatherer
(E) agrarian

312. The program for developing countries that reduces their foreign debt and promotes local conservation funding is known as

(A) Green Revolution
(B) market gardening
(C) debt-for-nature swap
(D) sustainable planning
(E) cultivation exchange

313. Which of the following is NOT an example of Mediterranean agriculture?

(A) Oranges in Florida
(B) Lemons in California
(C) Raisins in Greece
(D) Olives in Italy
(E) Grapes in southwest Australia

314. Plants and animals that have been genetically adapted to suit human needs are considered

(A) feral
(B) cultivated
(C) primitive
(D) domesticated
(E) indigenous

315. Which of the following is a benefit of industrial agriculture?

(A) It uses fewer fossil fuels.
(B) It gives consumers more access to food.
(C) It conserves water through irrigation.
(D) It increases the number of farming jobs.
(E) It decreases the amount of chemical fertilizers running off farm fields.

316. Slash-and-burn is an example of what type of agriculture practice?

(A) Sustainable farming
(B) Pastoral agriculture
(C) Collective farming
(D) Subsistence farming
(E) Plantation agriculture

317. A crop grown for profit is called a

(A) staple crop
(B) domesticated crop
(C) food crop
(D) primary crop
(E) cash crop

318. Which of the following is NOT true about market gardening?

(A) It sells goods directly to consumers and restaurants.
(B) It requires more manual labor than mechanized farming.
(C) It produces a diverse variety of crops.
(D) It relies on monoculture production.
(E) It operates on a relatively small scale.

319. Which of the following is NOT a cause of desertification?

(A) Overgrazing by animals

(B) Off-road vehicles increasing soil loss in drylands

(C) Overcultivation of semiarid lands

(D) Policies favoring nomadic herding over sedentary farming

(E) Irrigation resulting in salinization

320. Which of the following is a practice of an extractive industry?

(A) Cutting timber and forest regeneration

(B) Mining for copper

(C) Horse breeding

(D) Growing soybeans

(E) Fishing for salmon

321. Which of the following is an argument made by Carl Sauer?

(A) Agrarian societies increased biodiversity in their homelands.

(B) The spread of universal faiths is a result of crop surplus.

(C) Natural landscapes have been indirectly altered by human activity.

(D) Nomadic people of the grasslands first domesticated crops.

(E) The shift from horticulture to agriculture resulted in increased male activity in farming.

322. A suitcase farm is defined as

(A) a commercial farm where no one lives and that is farmed by migratory workers

(B) temporarily cultivated land that is abandoned after several seasons

(C) land to and from which seasonal pasture animals are moved throughout the year

(D) a farm where crops are grown for human consumption rather than for animals

(E) commercial production of fruit from orchards

323. The early agricultural location model suggests that

(A) grain crops should lie closest to the market center to maximize profits

(B) ranching should lie closest to the market center to maximize profits

(C) timber and firewood should lie near the wilderness to maximize profits

(D) vegetable farms should lie far from the market center to maximize profits

(E) dairying should lie closest to the market center to maximize profits

324. What is an older system of land surveying that relies on descriptions of land ownership and natural features such as streams and trees?

(A) Metes and bounds

(B) Township and range

(C) Universal transverse mercator (UTM)

(D) Long lots

(E) Nucleated

325. The farming of oysters is an example of

(A) polyculture

(B) hydroponics

(C) aeroponics

(D) aquaculture

(E) waterlogging

326. A direct result of the U.S. farm crisis in the 1980s was

(A) more jobs available in the farming industry

(B) less food available for consumption

(C) a decrease in the number of small farms

(D) increased price of crops for consumers

(E) higher profits for farmers

327. To reduce the risk of depleting the soil of nutrients, a farmer decides to plant legumes in a field that previously grew corn. This practice is called

(A) crop rotation

(B) companion cropping

(C) succession cropping

(D) double cropping

(E) no-till planting

328. Limiting the amount of timber cut from a forest to prevent forest depletion, thus ensuring its production for future use, is an example of

(A) intensive subsistence agriculture

(B) sustainable yield

(C) nonrenewable resources

(D) specialization

(E) an adaptive strategy

329. Which of the following is NOT an example of a luxury crop?

(A) Tea

(B) Cacao

(C) Tobacco

(D) Wool

(E) Coffee

330. Which of the following is true regarding the growing season?

(A) The Northern Hemisphere has a longer growing season than the Southern Hemisphere.

(B) Areas near the poles have longer growing seasons than regions near the equator.

(C) The Southern Hemisphere has a longer growing season than the Northern Hemisphere.

(D) Lands near the equator have longer growing seasons than at the poles.

(E) Growing seasons are the same around the world.

331. All of the following are true of the Green Revolution EXCEPT

(A) Food crises were prevented in some parts of the world.

(B) Crops are grown without the use of synthetic pesticides or fertilizers.

(C) Crops are grown from hybridized seeds to increase yields.

(D) The high price of seeds and fertilizers perpetuates socioeconomic divides.

(E) Farmers must buy new seeds each year.

332. Which of the following is an example of agribusiness?

(A) Manufacturing clothing from cotton

(B) Selling handwoven wool rugs

(C) Processing crops into canned food

(D) Cutting trees for lumber

(E) Mining coal for energy

333. The enclosure movement changed farming in England during the 18th century by

(A) consolidating the many small farms into fewer large farms

(B) encouraging land closest to villages to be farmed rather than land in the rural countryside

(C) requiring pens and corrals for any livestock within city limits

(D) restricting herding and grazing to specific areas

(E) initiating building codes for barns and silos

334. Which of the following is NOT a major hearth of agriculture development and animal domestication?

(A) Western Africa

(B) Central America

(C) Southern Europe

(D) Southeast Asia

(E) Northwest South America

335. The Middle East is known as the Fertile Crescent because

(A) it is the largest modern exporter of cereal crops

(B) it developed new farming machinery that revolutionized modern agriculture

(C) historically it has had a high birth rate

(D) it offered biodiversity in a complex marshland ecosystem

(E) it was one of the first areas of sedentary farming and urban society

336. Which of the following agricultural practices most closely followed hunting and gathering?

(A) Swidden, or slash-and-burn

(B) Pastoralism

(C) Intensive agriculture

(D) Extensive agriculture

(E) Commercial farms

337. All of the following are true of crop rotation systems EXCEPT

(A) Early crop rotation systems were mentioned in ancient Roman literature.

(B) George Washington Carver helped popularize the use of peanuts in crop rotation in the United States.

(C) Most crop rotation systems involve planting three or four crops in an area in succession to preserve yields and nutrient levels.

(D) Crop rotation nearly always increases the need for artificial fertilizers.

(E) The four-field crop rotation system was a key to the 18th-century British Agricultural Revolution.

338. Feedlots are an example of what kind of farming?

(A) Intensive cultivation

(B) Free-range farming

(C) Labor-intensive farming

(D) Subsistence farming

(E) Shifting cultivation

339. Which of the following is true of the environmental impact of organic farming?

(A) The positive impact of organic farming on the environment is negligible because it is far less energy efficient than conventional farming.

(B) Organic farms are very beneficial to the environment because they do not use tractors or other internal combustion farm equipment.

(C) Organic farming has a positive environmental impact because organic farming helps sustain diverse ecosystems due to the lack of synthetic pesticides.

(D) The overall effect of organic farming on the environment is negative because very few crops can be effectively produced with organic farming.

(E) Organic farms are harmful to the environment because they produce far more waste than conventional farms.

340. All of the following are true according to the von Thünen model of agricultural land EXCEPT

(A) There is a certain distance beyond which agricultural activity is not profitable.

(B) Land values decrease with distance from urban markets.

(C) Rents are highest close to urban markets.

(D) Dairy farms are located close to the city because of the perishability of dairy products.

(E) Forests for fuel and timber production could be located in any of the four rings.

341. Which of the following best characterizes the Green Revolution?

(A) The Green Revolution introduced new growing techniques that required less reliance on pesticides and technology.

(B) The Green Revolution resulted in increased biodiversity worldwide, especially in places where monocropping and high-yield varietals were prevalent.

(C) The Green Revolution was able to increase crop yields and food production in many locations throughout the world, but its impact on the environment, geopolitics, and the world economy has yet to be fully understood.

(D) There have been no major famines since the agricultural practices of the Green Revolution took hold in the 1960s.

(E) Much more land was put under cultivation during the Green Revolution, and this, rather than the development of high-yield varietals, was responsible for the increase in food production from 1960 to 1985.

342. All of the following were features of the British Agricultural Revolution between the 17th and 19th centuries EXCEPT

(A) the drawing away of workers from factories growing up during the same period in the Industrial Revolution

(B) the invention of mechanical farm implements like Jethro Tull's seed drill

(C) the development of four-field crop rotation

(D) an enclosure movement for livestock

(E) the use of technology and advancements from other areas of Europe and America

343. People who engage in subsistence agriculture

(A) concentrate on two or three crops that can be sold for cash at the end of the season

(B) regularly make purchases in the marketplace

(C) never use slash-and-burn techniques

(D) may engage in intensive cultivation in areas of high population density

(E) are practicing a relatively new form of agriculture

344. All of the following are true of the beginning of agriculture EXCEPT

(A) Evidence for domestication of fruit trees does not appear until thousands of years after the beginning of agriculture.

(B) Evidence for domestication of the founder crops of agriculture has been dated to about 9500 BCE in the Fertile Crescent.

(C) Agriculture grew up in many areas of the world between 9500 BCE and about 7000 BCE.

(D) By the Bronze Age, agriculture was being practiced on a fairly large scale in many parts of the world.

(E) Early animal domestication arose at nearly the same time as the earliest evidence of plant domestication.

345. Transhumance can best be described as

(A) the use of feedlots to raise livestock

(B) the seasonal movement of people and livestock over to different vertical elevations for the purposes of grazing

(C) a practice by which crops are rotated in a four-field system

(D) the use of animal manure as fertilizer in intensive cultivation

(E) long cattle drives in the 19th century to move stock from pastures to railheads in Kansas, Texas, and Missouri

346. Agriculture practices have evolved over human history due to advancing technologies and knowledge.

(A) Describe the First Agricultural Revolution and discuss how it changed agriculture practices.

(B) Describe the Second Agricultural Revolution and discuss how it changed agriculture practices.

(C) Describe the Third Agricultural Revolution and discuss how it changed agriculture practices.

347. Desertification is the end result of a long, gradual process.

(A) Identify factors leading to desertification.

(B) Explain how salinization destroys arable land.

(C) Explain how soil conservation can create sustainable agriculture.

348. Genetically modifying organisms for human benefit is a hotly debated topic.

    (A) Explain how genetically engineered crops can benefit humans.

    (B) Identify and explain possible drawbacks to genetic modification of food crops.

    (C) Discuss the future of biotechnology in relation to agriculture: will its influence continue to grow, or will it wane in favor of organic farming? Support your opinion with examples.

CHAPTER 6

Industrialization and Economic Development

349. In the 200 years following the Industrial Revolution, heavy industry was found in all of the following locations EXCEPT

(A) North America
(B) Russia
(C) France
(D) east Asia
(E) northern Africa

350. Service-based economies are focused on all of the following EXCEPT

(A) telecommunications
(B) tourism
(C) marketing
(D) sales
(E) mining

351. Export-processing zones are most often located in

(A) periphery and semi-periphery regions of developing nations
(B) areas with high tax rates
(C) countries with low rates of unemployment
(D) regions inaccessible by mass transit
(E) residential areas of developed nations

352. Deindustrialization occurred at the national level in Great Britain when heavy industry was moved to locations with

(A) greater access to major ports

(B) lower production costs

(C) a more educated population

(D) economies more geared toward tertiary economic activities

(E) higher industrial-economic development

353. According to Rostow's stages of development, which of the following is true?

(A) All countries will eventually pass through each of the five stages of economic development.

(B) The colonial legacy will impede a country's economic growth.

(C) Foreign investment is a necessary precondition for economic development in the second stage.

(D) Countries might not pass through each of the stages in a linear manner.

(E) Deindustrialization is accounted for in the fifth and final stage.

354. In the core-periphery model of global economic patterns, all of Africa is included in the periphery EXCEPT

(A) Zimbabwe

(B) Morocco

(C) South Africa

(D) Liberia

(E) Egypt

355. Which of the following groups of American cities is part of the Rust Belt?

(A) Detroit, Buffalo, and Cleveland

(B) San Jose, Palo Alto, and Cupertino

(C) St. Louis, Little Rock, and Oklahoma City

(D) Atlanta, Augusta, and Knoxville

(E) Albuquerque, Tucson, and Phoenix

356. Mexico's system of maquiladoras is located

(A) along the coast of the Pacific Ocean

(B) on the Baja Peninsula

(C) on the Yucatan Peninsula

(D) along the Mexico–United States border

(E) in the areas surrounding Mexico City

357. China leads newly industrialized countries in terms of demographic transition mostly due to

(A) its one-child policy

(B) rapid urbanization

(C) advanced infrastructure

(D) low labor costs

(E) high per capita income

358. Which of the following encourages the input of cash from foreign countries without the export of goods?

(A) Agricultural development

(B) Tourism

(C) Free-trade agreements

(D) E-commerce

(E) Development of infrastructure

359. Which of the following characterizes a developing nation?

(A) An economy based on agriculture

(B) A hard-line Communist government

(C) The lack of a formal government

(D) A service-based economy

(E) A government controlled by the military

360. Offshore financial centers allow companies and individuals to

(A) avoid high taxes in the countries where they conduct business

(B) spread their wealth to less developed countries

(C) take advantage of low labor costs

(D) pay lower banking fees

(E) do business in second-world countries

361. The process where manufacturers manage inventory by keeping only what they need immediately on hand and rely on communication and transportation to provide more resources or goods as needed is called

(A) footloose industry

(B) least-cost location

(C) break-of-bulk

(D) just-in-time delivery

(E) de-industrialization

362. Which of the following is an example of what some Western states refer to as a second-world country?

(A) Brazil

(B) South Africa

(C) Sierra Leone

(D) Cuba

(E) South Korea

363. Which of the following was a trigger for deindustrialization in Asian countries such as Japan and South Korea in the late 1990s?

(A) The Asian economic crisis

(B) An increase in the cost of labor

(C) Withdrawal of foreign investments

(D) The outsourcing of labor to North America

(E) A sudden decline in population

364. NAFTA allowed for free trade among which of the following?

(A) North America and South America

(B) Canada, the United States, and Mexico

(C) Great Britain, Ireland, and France

(D) Russia and the former Soviet states

(E) Iran, Iraq, and Saudi Arabia

365. According to Immanuel Wallerstein's world-system theory, the modern network of global economic interdependence and competition began

    (A) when European nations began exploring outside of their continent in the 1600s

    (B) with the spread of the Industrial Revolution from northern Europe to Asia

    (C) in the early 1990s with the collapse of the Soviet Union and fall of communism

    (D) after the United States resumed trade with Great Britain following the American Revolution

    (E) with the spread of capitalism at the end of the 19th century

366. Goods are classified as durable or nondurable based on the

    (A) amount of energy required to manufacture the goods

    (B) amount paid for the goods by consumers

    (C) amount of time a product can be used

    (D) complexity of the manufacturing process used to produce the goods

    (E) availability of the resources used to produce the goods

367. All of the following are trade agreements between two or more countries EXCEPT

    (A) NAFTA

    (B) SADC

    (C) G-3

    (D) CEFTA

    (E) OPEC

368. Which of the following is an example of quaternary economic activity?

    (A) Entertainment

    (B) Research and development

    (C) Oil production

    (D) Agriculture

    (E) Transportation

369. The Human Development Index is a measure of both economic production and

(A) social indicators
(B) population density
(C) unemployment rates
(D) income per capita
(E) income disparity

370. When compared to fossil fuels, alternative energy sources generally

(A) create more waste
(B) are more expensive
(C) require less investment
(D) are less sustainable
(E) are more efficient

371. Service and high-tech industry jobs offer all of the following benefits over manufacturing jobs EXCEPT

(A) higher pay
(B) less pollution
(C) safer working conditions
(D) higher standard of living
(E) shorter workweeks

372. Deglomeration occurs when a location

(A) experiences a natural disaster
(B) does not have a large enough labor force
(C) is saturated with businesses offering similar services
(D) sees an increase in large firms moving in
(E) experiences a rapid loss of manufacturing activity

373. The Gini coefficient measures the income disparity between

(A) the wealthiest and poorest population groups in a country
(B) men and women throughout developing countries
(C) residents of urban and rural areas in a country
(D) workers in different industries in the same country
(E) members of the middle class in European countries

374. Which of the following is an example of a bulk-reducing industry?

(A) Water bottling
(B) Car manufacturing
(C) Steelmaking
(D) Furniture manufacturing
(E) Food packaging

375. Italy and Kuwait are examples of countries with

(A) high GNP and low gender equity
(B) low per capita income and high GNP
(C) high HDI and low unemployment rate
(D) low Gini coefficient and high gender equity
(E) high population density and low HDI

376. All of the following are Old Asian Tigers EXCEPT

(A) Japan
(B) South Korea
(C) Taiwan
(D) China
(E) Singapore

377. The United States and Great Britain invested in manufacturing industries in the Old Asian Tiger countries in order to

(A) stop the spread of communism by establishing a free market
(B) rebuild the economies of these countries following World War I
(C) open up new markets for manufacturing companies in the West
(D) preserve economic ties created in colonial times
(E) make a profit on loans given to these countries

378. A location along a transport route where goods must be transferred from one carrier to another—for example, from a ship to a train—is called

(A) outsourcing
(B) technology transfer
(C) the break-of-bulk point
(D) carrier efficiency
(E) economies of scale

379. All of the following are examples of renewable energy sources EXCEPT

(A) natural gas
(B) solar energy
(C) geothermal energy
(D) hydropower
(E) biomass

380. Foreign development aid from developed countries to developing countries is

(A) only given through the World Bank
(B) only given in extreme circumstances
(C) used only for for-profit investment
(D) given in exchange for military aid
(E) not expected to be paid back

381. Which of the following is an example of a developing country that has experienced an economic crisis and is now classified as at a lower stage of development?

(A) China
(B) North Korea
(C) Sierra Leone
(D) Argentina
(E) Kuwait

382. The shift of industry to developing countries has resulted in

(A) tighter trade restrictions across the globe
(B) higher unemployment in developing countries
(C) a lower standard of living in developing countries
(D) an industrial decline in the United States and Europe
(E) a more robust economy in the United States and Europe

383. Henry Ford insisted on paying laborers high wages for unskilled work in order to ensure that workers

(A) could afford health care so that they could work
(B) would gain skills and leave his factory for other jobs
(C) would organize themselves to form labor unions
(D) could afford to buy the products they produced
(E) did not sell trade secrets to other corporations

384. In a right-to-work state, workers cannot

    (A) negotiate a contract with an employer without a union
    (B) join a union if their employer forbids it
    (C) be fired without proof of cause
    (D) be paid overtime for more than 40 hours of work a week
    (E) be forced to join a union as a condition of employment

385. In cottage industries, manufacturing takes place

    (A) in large factories
    (B) in homes
    (C) within designated industrial areas
    (D) on farms in rural areas
    (E) in large shopping centers

386. Which area of the United States is known as a megalopolis?

    (A) The Mid-Atlantic
    (B) The Eastern Great Lakes
    (C) The Southwest
    (D) The South
    (E) The Pacific Northwest

387. Which of the following former Soviet nations controls much of the agricultural production and coal deposits formerly held by the USSR?

    (A) Belarus
    (B) Ukraine
    (C) Estonia
    (D) Lithuania
    (E) Latvia

388. Which Chinese city is home to one of the world's largest industrial parks?

    (A) Beijing
    (B) Chengdu
    (C) Shanghai
    (D) Wuhan
    (E) Yenchuan

389. In a Socialist economy, the government controls the prices of basic goods and services in order to ensure that

(A) no one corporation gains too much power
(B) the government has enough money to pay for defense
(C) all citizens have access to essential services
(D) everyone who wants a job has a job
(E) everyone has an incentive to be successful

390. According to dependency theory, some countries allow a large number of citizens to live in poverty in order to

(A) keep labor costs down and bring in new industry
(B) allow an elite class to control all economic resources
(C) avoid spending government resources on social programs
(D) create a large unskilled labor force to promote industrialization
(E) stop rapid population growth and urbanization

391. Which of the following is a characteristic of a downward transition area?

(A) High unemployment rates
(B) A large tax base
(C) Population growth
(D) Rapid economic growth
(E) High cost of living

392. During the contagion stage of Richard Nolan's stages of growth model

(A) technology is used minimally
(B) technology begins to spread
(C) people become frustrated with technology
(D) practical uses for technology are developed
(E) technology is integrated into the workplace

393. Which region of the United States is currently experiencing upward transition?

(A) Pacific Northwest
(B) Rust Belt
(C) Mid-Atlantic states
(D) Great Plains
(E) Sunbelt

394. Expendable income is what is left after

(A) taxes have been paid

(B) all necessary bills have been paid

(C) housing costs have been paid

(D) energy and transportation costs have been paid

(E) food and utility costs have been paid

395. The idea that some people have more access to and are better able to use technology is called

(A) the technology gap

(B) contagion theory of technology

(C) technology transfer process

(D) maturity stage of technology

(E) technology deficiency

396. The northern parts of Alaska, which contain crude oil resources, can be classified as which of the following under the core-periphery model?

(A) Downward transition

(B) Upward transition

(C) Resource frontier

(D) Industrial core

(E) Export processing zone

397. In China, special economic zones have been set up to accommodate

(A) industry funded by local investors

(B) mining in areas rich in natural resources

(C) headquarters for foreign companies

(D) rural farms and cottage industries

(E) transportation hubs

398. The optimistic viewpoint of economic development is based on which of the following principles?

(A) There is an abundance of both renewable and nonrenewable sources of energy and these resources can be shared.

(B) There is enough energy available in the form of fossil fuels to meet the needs of the planet for many millennia.

(C) Within 100 years all of the world's energy needs will be met by alternative sources of energy.

(D) The demand for energy will increase as the world's population increases, and this demand can be met with alternative energy.

(E) The world's population is on the decline, and the current energy supply is adequate.

399. The level of wealth and life enjoyment that a person holds, which is sometimes measured by metrics such as the average real gross domestic product per capita, is called

(A) cost of living

(B) life expectancy

(C) literacy

(D) standard of living

(E) human development index

400. In which of the following regions is life expectancy the lowest?

(A) Northern Europe

(B) The Middle East

(C) Southeast Asia

(D) Sub-Saharan Africa

(E) Central America

401. Which of the following is the basic industry for Silicon Valley in California?

(A) Farming

(B) Steel manufacturing

(C) Computer equipment manufacturing

(D) Milling

(E) Food packaging

402. The Eastern Great Lakes region, which has included some important areas of industrial development, includes all of the following cities EXCEPT

(A) Niagara Falls
(B) Pittsburgh
(C) Toronto
(D) Buffalo
(E) Boston

403. Literacy rate, life expectancy, and infant mortality rate are used to calculate

(A) gross national product
(B) Physical Quality of Life Index
(C) standard of living
(D) Gender-Related Development Index
(E) Multidimensional Poverty Index

404. The gross domestic product per capita is a measure of the total goods and services produced by a country divided by that country's

(A) unemployment rate
(B) gross national product
(C) total population
(D) number of corporations
(E) total number of exports

405. Which of the following is the most energy-efficient method of transportation per mile of travel?

(A) Trains
(B) Diesel trucks
(C) Ships
(D) Airplanes
(E) Personal vehicles

406. Shopping malls are an example of

(A) urbanization
(B) deglomeration
(C) agglomeration
(D) cumulative causation
(E) gentrification

407. Brain drain occurs when

(A) young people leave their home country for education and do not return

(B) teachers are underpaid and leave education to work in other industries

(C) a workforce is undereducated and can only perform low-skill jobs

(D) educational facilities close due to lack of funding and support from the government

(E) girls and women do not have the same access to education as boys and men

408. As a result of the treaty Japan signed ending World War II and forbidding Japan from building its military, the government was able to

(A) promote industrial development through direct investment

(B) force people who used to be in the military to work in factories

(C) lower taxes and put more expendable income in the hands of consumers

(D) move from a manufacturing-based economy to a service-based economy

(E) spend more money on importing foreign-produced goods

409. All of the following are true of e-commerce EXCEPT

(A) Many e-commerce transactions are transactions to purchase virtual items like premium Web content.

(B) Telephone banking and ATMs also fit under the umbrella of e-commerce.

(C) Increased competition from e-commerce has driven many traditional retailers out of business.

(D) The growth of e-commerce as a segment of the world economy is not expected to increase significantly in the next decade.

(E) E-commerce gives consumers the advantage of having more information about products and prices.

410. A free trade zone is an area where

(A) the normal trade laws of a country, such as tariffs, bureaucratic requirements, and quotas, are eliminated in hopes of stimulating foreign trade and industry

(B) large open markets are set up in poor countries for the exchange of international currencies

(C) black market trade is carried out under government supervision

(D) ideas are exchanged in an academic setting to increase the academic activity of the country

(E) people bring agricultural products for trade and barter

411. All of the following are true of the Industrial Revolution EXCEPT

(A) Technological advancements such as steam power and machine tools helped make the Industrial Revolution possible.

(B) Despite social and economic problems, standards of living and incomes increased for most people in industrializing countries.

(C) The Industrial Revolution marked the transition from manual labor and draft animals to mechanization.

(D) One of the first industries transformed by the Industrial Revolution was the textile industry.

(E) Industrialization happened nearly simultaneously in most areas of the world in the 18th century.

412. An industry that could be located anywhere without ramifications such as increased delivery times or lack of raw materials is called

(A) a heavy industry

(B) a labor-intensive industry

(C) a service industry

(D) a primary industry

(E) a footloose industry

413. All of the following are criticisms of using gross domestic product (GDP) as a measure of standard of living for residents of a country EXCEPT

(A) It does not measure the distribution of wealth.

(B) It is possible for GDP to increase and for real incomes in a country to decline under certain conditions.

(C) It is measured in a consistent way worldwide.

(D) It does not take the nonmonetary economy into account.

(E) It does not measure economic externalities.

414. All of the following are true of the Human Development Index EXCEPT

(A) Most countries that score very high on the scale are located in North America and Europe.

(B) Many low-HDI countries are located in sub-Saharan Africa.

(C) The HDI measures factors such as life expectancy, literacy, education level, and standard of living.

(D) Ecology and the environment are strongly considered in the HDI calculations.

(E) The United States loses points on the HDI because its education level and literacy rates are lower than countries like Norway and Canada.

415. Unlike the rural poor in developing countries, the urban poor of cities like Mumbai, India, and Jakarta, Indonesia,

(A) enjoy a higher standard of living than those living in rural areas

(B) enjoy higher employment rates than those living in rural areas

(C) find better housing opportunities than those living in rural areas

(D) are better educated than their rural counterparts

(E) are far more likely to live in overcrowded, squalid, and unsanitary conditions

416. In Immanuel Wallerstein's world-system theory, core countries in Europe in the 15th and 16th centuries had an advantage in commerce and used this to

(A) subjugate and colonize peripheral and semiperipheral countries

(B) develop equal trading relationships with peripheral countries

(C) share technologies and economic practices with semiperipheral countries

(D) establish trading networks free of trade barriers with other core countries

(E) integrate the peoples of peripheral and semiperipheral countries into their societies

417. Industries with material orientation are

(A) those that can operate efficiently in any location
(B) most advantageously located near their source materials
(C) those that combine large numbers of different materials to make one product
(D) heavily dependent on migrant labor and advantageously located near international borders
(E) those that service other industries, such as petroleum or agriculture

418. Alfred Weber's least cost theory takes into account all of the following EXCEPT

(A) locating markets close to source materials
(B) transportation costs
(C) weight of raw materials
(D) agglomeration costs
(E) consumer demand for the finished product

419. All of the following are true of globalization EXCEPT

(A) Access to technology can determine the extent to which countries can participate in the global economy.
(B) Globalization involves the division of labor on an international scale.
(C) Proponents of globalization argue that increased economic integration will promote world peace.
(D) Globalization involves not only economic activity but also cultural exchange, migration, trade, and technology.
(E) Globalization has affected all areas of the world in very similar ways and at comparable rates.

420. One of the possible negative results of ecotourism is

(A) offsetting the destruction of natural habitats
(B) educating the populace about environmental conservation
(C) allowing people a way to earn money without engaging in slash-and-burn agriculture
(D) preventing the displacement of indigenous cultures and peoples
(E) attracting a younger, more eco-conscious tourism clientele

421. The British Agricultural Revolution and the Industrial Revolution were tied together in that

(A) The Agricultural Revolution produced a surplus population of displaced agricultural workers who provided labor for factories.

(B) Working conditions in factories during the Industrial Revolution drove workers to agricultural jobs in large numbers.

(C) Mechanization occurred much more quickly in agriculture than it did in industry during this period.

(D) The cost of food rose during the Agricultural Revolution, which resulted in severe malnutrition among industrial workers.

(E) The Industrial Revolution and Agricultural Revolution shared only a time period, but not technology or ideas.

422. Cell phones and the rise of social networks have led to all of the following EXCEPT

(A) a rapid flow of information across the globe

(B) equal access to information and technology across the globe

(C) political revolutions in countries dominated by despots

(D) rapid development in emerging economies

(E) cultural exchange between countries and people separated by distance

423. Under the balanced growth approach to economic development,

(A) states focus all their economic growth on one or two major regions

(B) economic growth is mainly centered in cities and not in the rural areas

(C) the primary industries are all owned and operated by the state

(D) economic investment is spread equally throughout all regions of a country

(E) high tariffs encourage the growth of some industries at the expense of others

424. All of these are industries where there is a situation factor that makes it advantageous for the factory to be close to the end market EXCEPT

(A) cars
(B) copper
(C) bottled beverages
(D) single-market industries
(E) dairy

425. All of the following are true of maquiladoras EXCEPT

(A) The North American Free Trade Agreement spurred the growth of maquiladoras in Mexico.
(B) Globalization has increased competition for maquiladoras in Mexico.
(C) Because of the North American Free Trade Agreement, maquiladoras are not subject to any Mexican taxes.
(D) U.S. firms take advantage of more lenient Mexican labor laws and cheaper wages by using the maquiladoras.
(E) China's special economic areas are a big threat to the maquiladoras because they provide cheaper labor in some cases.

426. In a bulk-gaining industry

(A) companies make money buying and selling bulky items
(B) companies assemble products whose weight is greater after assembly
(C) companies make weight-gain supplements
(D) maquiladoras provide the labor force
(E) production centers are far from their markets

427. The development of the core-periphery model led to hundreds of years of European domination of world markets.

(A) Discuss the ways Europeans excluded nonmember countries from core benefits.
(B) Peripheral countries have long been excluded from access to technological advances. How have cell phones and the Internet begun to even out the playing field for developing countries? Support your opinion with examples.
(C) Semiperipheral countries were exploited by core countries. How did that in turn affect peripheral countries?

428. Cottage industry has become a popular idea again. Many seek to reclaim the balance of nature through the use of renewable resources and a small ecological footprint.

(A) How can cottage industries compete with multinational corporations?

(B) Use of computers has led to the rise of many home-based businesses. How can this trend benefit the communities in which they are based?

(C) Burt's Bees is an example of a company that has outgrown its cottage industry beginnings. Yet it still employs ecological conservation. Are the two mutually exclusive? Provide examples to back up your argument.

CHAPTER 7

Cities and Urban Land Use

429. In the past, many urban areas were viewed as "male spaces" because women had comparatively few opportunities to

(A) produce children and help raise families
(B) find employment and buy property
(C) use public transportation systems
(D) maintain a network of female friends
(E) barter and sell goods

430. Today, city planners work to create healthy urban environments by designing neighborhoods and streets that allow residents to

(A) obtain organic foods
(B) engage in regular exercise
(C) drive without obstacles
(D) easily access health clinics of all sizes
(E) commute quickly to schools and workplaces

431. Under the bid rent theory,

(A) areas easily accessible to the city center earn the highest rents
(B) the most physically attractive locations earn the highest rents
(C) landlords will accept bids for renting commercial real estate
(D) the lowest rents are in the urban city centers
(E) businesses look for the cheapest rents without caring about location

432. In a futuristic version of Hoyt's sector model, low-income populations would be most likely to live close to

(A) industrial canals
(B) high-speed rail lines
(C) green spaces and parks
(D) pedestrian walkways
(E) wind farms

433. The gravity model, which can be used to calculate the bonds between different urban centers, assumes that two cities located close together

  (A) would attract more people than two cities located far apart
  (B) would not attract a large number of people
  (C) would only attract people to the larger of the two cities
  (D) would attract equal numbers of people to each city
  (E) would attract fewer people than the residential population of both cities combined

434. Residents of edge cities and suburban areas have long depended on automobiles and public transportation to access

  (A) performing arts centers in large cities
  (B) educational opportunities in large cities
  (C) jobs in large cities
  (D) places of religious worship in large cities
  (E) family networks in large cities

435. A *greenbelt policy* encourages a city to curb the amount of construction on a city's edges to encourage growth in

  (A) the city's suburbs
  (B) the city's industrial zones
  (C) the city's transportation networks
  (D) the city's waterfront district
  (E) the city's core

436. The political powers of a city council are typically outlined in

  (A) the city commission's handbook
  (B) the platform of the city's controlling political party
  (C) the state's labor code
  (D) the federal constitution
  (E) the state's constitution

437. In the United States, it has been demonstrated that a sudden influx of wealth into an urban ghetto typically leads to

  (A) a drop in the number of women-owned businesses in the ghetto
  (B) the ghetto's transformation into a commuter zone
  (C) further segregation and the persistence of the ghetto
  (D) desegregation and economic development within the ghetto
  (E) reunification of extended families throughout the ghetto

438. In many American cities, public transportation and emergency response services must be improved within the next 25 years primarily to serve

(A) the aging Baby Boomer population
(B) inner-city college students
(C) commuters from suburban areas
(D) industrial workers from rural areas
(E) Generation X service workers

439. Landless residents of large cities often band together to address their concerns through political demonstrations that may later solidify into

(A) ad hoc committees
(B) grassroots organizations
(C) trade associations
(D) civic associations
(E) neighborhood block clubs

440. When a city is NOT designed to be sustainable and eco-friendly, it has the potential to become

(A) a center of "lost space"
(B) part of the public realm
(C) a suburban ghetto
(D) an urban heat island
(E) an eco-village

441. The 1970s and 1980s departure of Caucasian middle- and high-income families from urban areas to outlying areas, termed *white flight*, was characterized primarily as

(A) a social movement
(B) a political movement
(C) an eco-movement
(D) a religious movement
(E) a racial movement

442. Housing cooperatives present a unique housing option for many urban residents, as they are often

(A) presidentially controlled and state-owned
(B) city-controlled and privately owned
(C) democratically controlled and community-owned
(D) government-controlled and individually owned
(E) corporate-controlled and privately owned

443. Opponents of *automobile dependency* in cities argue that traffic congestion creates a constant demand for

(A) bigger, more streamlined roads
(B) an increased number of bicycle paths
(C) more modern light rail systems
(D) evenly distributed office parks
(E) more traffic lights and pedestrian crossings

444. One reason cities develop affordable urban housing and working spaces is to encourage an increase in the number of

(A) traditional industrial jobs
(B) transportation-related jobs
(C) arts and creative jobs
(D) agricultural jobs
(E) information sector jobs

445. Increasingly, residents of *gated communities*, both within cities and in suburbs, are commonly recognized as having

(A) low incomes and poor lifestyles
(B) high incomes and elite lifestyles
(C) median incomes and middle-class lifestyles
(D) no incomes and varying lifestyles
(E) varying incomes and unconventional lifestyles

446. Many American cities developed unevenly between the Industrial Revolution and the late 1900s because developers and investors rejected city plans that allowed

(A) businesses and housing to be close together
(B) businesses and housing to be separated by a rural barrier
(C) businesses to be located in strip malls
(D) housing to be in outlying suburban areas
(E) big-box retailers to build stores within city limits

447. The concentric zone model demonstrates a way that urban residents were able to gradually move up economically and socially by allowing them

(A) to migrate progressively away from the working-class zone
(B) to migrate progressively away from the residential zone
(C) to migrate progressively away from the commuter zone
(D) to migrate progressively away from the transitional zone
(E) to migrate progressively away from the central business district

448. In Harris and Ullman's multiple-nuclei model, a city could be understood as lacking a central business district if

(A) similar industries were located in one large business park
(B) different industries were located in one large business park
(C) similar industries were scattered throughout the main city's edge cities
(D) different industries were located throughout the city
(E) different industries were concentrated in one of the main city's suburbs

449. After World War II, the governments of many European nations countered urban housing shortages by building

(A) public housing in rural areas
(B) private residential towers within the city
(C) subsidized housing blocks within the city
(D) efficient urban highways
(E) private residential housing in commuter zones

450. Until recently, many transportation plans for urban areas failed to create space for environmentally friendly corridors for transportation such as

(A) highways and side streets
(B) overpasses for private bus lines
(C) waterways for freight ships
(D) pedestrian walkways and bicycle paths
(E) airspace for helicopters and private planes

451. As an urban neighborhood's socioeconomic status decreases, its residents are more likely to be denied the opportunity to

(A) enter into mortgages and receive home loans

(B) attend local public schools

(C) participate in city government meetings

(D) find employment in the city's central district

(E) commute to rural areas

452. Studies in urban areas such as Washington, DC, have indicated that when the number of high-wage jobs increases in the suburbs, the number of low-wage jobs is likely to rise

(A) in the suburbs

(B) in rural areas

(C) in neither the suburbs nor the central city

(D) in urban greenbelts

(E) in the central city

453. Many of today's emerging megacities, such as Rio de Janeiro and Guangzhou, are actually NOT one distinct city but

(A) a collection of highly populated religious centers

(B) multiple cities that have merged

(C) academic institutions located close to suburbs and edge cities

(D) a collection of company towns set up by major industries

(E) a ring of commuter towns

454. In developing nations such as Egypt, large numbers of individuals leave rural areas to find work in

(A) agricultural communes

(B) academic centers

(C) large cities

(D) sites for religious pilgrims

(E) small and medium-size cities

455. Central place theory lost ground in the 20th century as city networks came to be seen as determining the importance of cities more than

(A) industries within the cities
(B) the size of the cities and less developed areas surrounding them
(C) people within the cities
(D) the size of the nation's largest cities
(E) the net economic growth generated by a region's suburbs

456. An excellent example of a primate city that serves as the focus of a country and its culture is

(A) Copenhagen, Denmark
(B) Marseilles, France
(C) Calgary, Canada
(D) Seattle, United States of America
(E) Tijuana, Mexico

457. Since the 1980s, there has been a trend to build suburbs and edge cities within the United States

(A) in mountainous, rocky areas
(B) along rural roads rather than major highways
(C) within and around historic districts of large cities
(D) increasingly closer to the central city
(E) increasingly farther away from the central city

458. In the city of Jerusalem, the concentric zone model can be modified to account for the presence of at least two central business districts for

(A) at least two different residential suburbs
(B) at least two similar homeless populations
(C) at least two different ethnic and religious populations
(D) at least two different government administrations
(E) at least two similar banking centers

459. Which of the following was a global city in the Western world during the time of the Greek and Roman Empires?

(A) Honolulu, United States of America
(B) Warsaw, Poland
(C) Almaty, Kazakhstan
(D) Alexandria, Egypt
(E) Arad, Israel

460. Christaller's central place theory, which provides a reason why a certain number of human settlements exist in an urban system, assumes that all consumers

(A) work at equal distances from one another
(B) are of the same ethnic background and have the same kinship patterns
(C) have the same income and shop in the same way
(D) travel to the farthest points possible to obtain luxury goods
(E) like to visit small shopping centers rather than large ones

461. The rank-size rule does NOT always fit when one considers the distribution of

(A) all of the citizens in a given country
(B) all of the cities in a given country
(C) all of the counties, provinces, or parishes within a given state
(D) all of the polities within a given region
(E) all of the hyperlocal systems of government within a given city

462. The concentric zone model is portrayed as a series of rings, with the outermost ring being the

(A) central business district
(B) factory zone
(C) commuter zone
(D) working-class zone
(E) zone of transition

463. A city seeking to reenergize an inactive central business district should take steps to

(A) plan events that will increase the number of residents and visitors within the district
(B) raze badly damaged historic buildings
(C) raise funds to build affordable housing units outside city limits
(D) separate residential and commercial activities
(E) raise property taxes to build parking lots for private cars throughout the neighborhood

464. In cities such as Chicago, individuals who take positions as members of a municipal council primarily engage in activities to

(A) make sure that funding is received for national parks within city limits
(B) make sure that city elections have candidates from at least two political parties
(C) make sure that the city government does not receive funds from the state government
(D) make sure that the mayor is reelected
(E) make sure that the city government functions correctly

465. During the 1950s, many urban American neighborhoods came to be segregated because of redlining, a practice engaged in by

(A) corporate real estate directors
(B) banks and other lending institutions
(C) independent surveyors
(D) civil rights activists
(E) renovators of historic homes

466. In the sector model, also known as the Hoyt model, it is proposed cities often grow outward from their centers because

(A) private cars will carry commuters in and out of the cities effectively

(B) there are not enough trails and bike paths within the city centers for residents who enjoy recreation

(C) major lines of transportation will carry commuters to outlying areas

(D) physical features such as lakes and rivers take up most of the space in the city centers

(E) many commercial activities in the city centers are eventually relocated to outlying residential areas

467. When a large city experiences a sudden spike in internal immigration, that is, citizens of that country begin flocking to the city, the population of the city is likely to include

(A) individuals who were formerly expatriates

(B) individuals who were formerly residents of rural areas and smaller cities

(C) individuals who were formerly members of rural collectives

(D) individuals with a high level of education

(E) individuals who are members of large extended families

468. Green building is a form of gentrification because it

(A) raises property values throughout a neighborhood

(B) creates an environment that encourages discrimination and prejudice

(C) restricts home ownership on the basis of sexual orientation

(D) requires cities to raise taxes on property owners

(E) maintains current zoning laws and regulations

469. During the Neolithic Revolution, the majority of cities originated in areas where the population was able to

(A) build underwater irrigation systems

(B) unite in polytheistic worship

(C) fight naval battles

(D) generate an agricultural surplus

(E) establish intercontinental trade routes

470. In Europe's Industrial Revolution, the rate of rural-urban migration increased as many members of which group left the fields for the factories?

(A) The barons
(B) The clergy
(C) The monarchy
(D) The merchants
(E) The peasants

471. The earliest cities appear to have developed from villages in which much of the population was already linked by

(A) complex kinship structures
(B) marine trade routes
(C) the slave trade
(D) a caste system
(E) paved roads and highways

472. What is a likely result of a rapid rise in the rate of rural-urban migration?

(A) An increase in the number of health problems in rural areas
(B) Increased literacy in rural areas
(C) Overcrowding in urban areas
(D) A decrease in the number of businesses in rural areas
(E) An increase in the number of children in urban areas

473. Many of the earliest cities grew rapidly because they were religious centers that attracted

(A) animal sacrifices
(B) priests and scribes
(C) pilgrims and pilgrimages
(D) the building of royal tombs
(E) trade by artisans

474. Many political leaders in the earliest cities funded centralized administrations by taxes collected on

(A) large building projects
(B) the sale of agricultural harvests
(C) the mentoring of apprentices through trade associations
(D) military training
(E) wild fish and game

475. When rural-urban migration is a cycle rather than a flow, it is likely because rural residents must return to rural areas to

(A) conduct religious rituals
(B) obtain an education
(C) hunt wild game
(D) raise agricultural crops
(E) undergo military training

476. A major problem facing modern megacities is

(A) the Sunbelt phenomena
(B) federal contracting
(C) air pollution
(D) long-distance trade
(E) the emergence of new ethnic communities

477. Global cities such as New York and London are characterized as such primarily because they are home to

(A) intense religious rituals
(B) major hospitals and medical centers
(C) historic ethnic neighborhoods
(D) immigrants who speak a variety of languages
(E) international business centers

478. In global cities, frequent displacement of minority populations with low incomes is often caused by the process of

(A) social reproduction
(B) urban blight
(C) gentrification
(D) rent control
(E) traffic congestion

479. Suburbanization causes cities to lose populations to areas surrounding them, which leads to

(A) congestion and racial tension
(B) decentralization and urban sprawl
(C) centralization and international immigration
(D) intense building in inner cities
(E) a shift from a manufacturing economy to an information-based service economy

480. A common exception to the rank-size rule occurs when the largest, or primate, city of a country is NOT much bigger than

(A) the rural areas outlying the primate city
(B) the larger cities of other countries
(C) the smaller cities of a country
(D) the capital city or district of a country
(E) the county in which the primate city exists

481. Christaller's central place theory explains that settlements will form in a triangular/hexagonal lattice, with the geometric shapes forming

(A) thresholds
(B) hierarchies of cities
(C) transport routes
(D) market areas
(E) uneven hinterlands

482. Edge cities typically grow on the borders of large urban areas at points near

(A) electrical and nuclear power plants
(B) schools and universities
(C) sports and recreation complexes
(D) major roads and airports
(E) navigable waterways

483. All of the following are part of Borchert's Epochs theory of urban transportation EXCEPT

(A) Auto-Air-Amenity Epoch
(B) Sail-Wagon Epoch
(C) Steel Rail Epoch
(D) Pedestrian Epoch
(E) High-Technology Epoch

484. In central place theory, range, or the maximum distance a consumer will travel to buy a good, is proportional to

(A) the cost of real property where the good is sold
(B) the cost of not obtaining the good
(C) the wholesale cost of the good
(D) the cost of living in the consumer's city
(E) the desire to obtain the good

485. The gravity model, used to predict flows of human activity between places, has been criticized for its inability to take into account

(A) frequent migration

(B) areas where people are underemployed

(C) the evolution of patterns

(D) natural disasters

(E) distance decay

486. In a concentric zone model, the zones outside the core are sized according to

(A) what people will pay for transportation

(B) what people will pay for the land

(C) what people will pay in taxes

(D) what people will pay for goods

(E) what people will pay for entertainment

487. The sector model, developed by Hoyt in the late 1930s, is accurate in explaining the growth of numerous industrial cities in

(A) Canada

(B) India

(C) Beijing

(D) Egypt

(E) Great Britain

488. Geographers Chauncy Harris and Edward Ullman developed their multiple-nuclei model during a time when many people began to use cars to navigate cities more easily. Which decade was it?

(A) 1930s

(B) 1890s

(C) 1910s

(D) 1940s

(E) 1970s

489. The simplest form of the gravity model looks at the interaction between

(A) two towns

(B) two megacities

(C) a city and the suburban areas that surround it

(D) a network of at least three towns

(E) a city and its hinterland

490. The multiple-nuclei model holds that a typical metropolitan area has multiple centers, one of which is the central business district (CBD) and the others of which are

(A) rural farms
(B) counties
(C) suburban downtowns
(D) shantytowns
(E) communes

491. As many cities discourage heavy industry from taking place within city limits, they work to motivate urban employers to increase the number of

(A) agricultural jobs
(B) student jobs
(C) part-time jobs
(D) seasonal jobs
(E) service jobs

492. *Job sprawl* involves the migration of jobs out of the urban cores of cities and into

(A) entertainment complexes
(B) the outermost rings surrounding cities
(C) gated communities
(D) sacred landscapes
(E) ports and waterways

493. In central place theory, the size of population required to make it economically feasible to provide certain services is called

(A) functional zonation
(B) the range
(C) the hinterland
(D) the tipping point
(E) the threshold

494. American cities experiencing deindustrialization have simultaneously been prone to an increase in

(A) modernization
(B) globalization
(C) ghettoization
(D) colonization
(E) suburbanization

495. Public housing is typically defined as affordable housing offered to low-income urban residents by

(A) international organizations
(B) local, state, and federal agencies
(C) private corporations
(D) religious organizations
(E) political parties

496. Housing in edge cities is often meant to create a semirural space in which houses and gardens are typically

(A) natural and unfenced
(B) extremely similar and minimalist
(C) sleek and modernist
(D) designed for agricultural use
(E) well manicured and gated

497. When a city's terrain is rugged and the city lacks basic infrastructure, which type of network offers the most flexibility for urban transportation?

(A) A grid of roads
(B) A rail line with many stations
(C) A grid of canals
(D) A set of pipelines
(E) A central airport

498. In the United States, cities in areas that have a high chance of being affected by natural disasters are required to develop emergency transit plans to

(A) help urban residents prepare for natural disasters
(B) eliminate the dangers posed by natural disasters
(C) determine where natural disasters might strike
(D) help urban residents evacuate in response to natural disasters
(E) minimize the effect of natural disasters

499. Use the following maps provided to determine Mexico City's role as a megacity within the country of Mexico, and as a global city in relation to the United States and Central America.

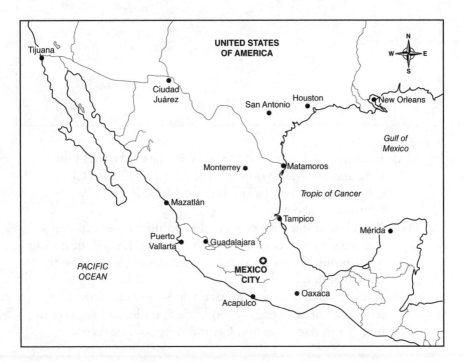

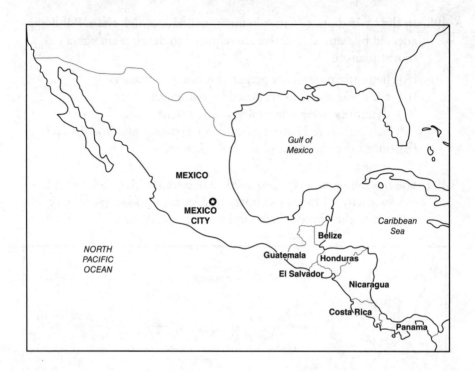

(A) Examine the location of Mexico City, or the Federal District, in relation to Mexico's other cities. Explain Mexico City's geographic limitations as a hub for Mexico's national commodity chain.

(B) Provide examples of two ways that economic ties between Mexico City and two of the larger cities in Texas, Houston and San Antonio, allow Mexico City's influence to spread to the United States.

(C) Identify three ways that Mexico City's location allows it to remain an urban node for production, trade, and finances to link North American and Central American markets.

500. City, local, state, and federal governments often must work to provide housing for individuals who are priced out of urban housing markets.

(A) Describe the types of housing governments should create for the following low-income groups: single-parent families, aging seniors, and single individuals with service-sector jobs.

(B) Provide examples of three ways that a city government could generate funds to improve existing affordable housing units.

(C) Explain three consequences of failing to build enough affordable housing for a large metropolitan area. These consequences may be social, economic, political, or environmental.

ANSWERS

Chapter 1: Key Geography Concepts

1. (D) A ratio of the number of items within a defined unit of area measures density. For example, human population density is typically measured according to the number of inhabitants per square mile or square kilometer of land. Because it is a ratio of quantity per unit of area, density always expresses a relative value.

2. (C) The *site* of Manhattan is best described as an island bordered by the Hudson and East Rivers. Site refers to a place's absolute location, often described in terms of its physical geography. Situation, on the other hand, refers to a place's location relative to external social relations, systems, or networks. All other available choices describe Manhattan's situation relative to other places.

3. (B) Spatial coordinates of latitude and longitude express absolute location. Absolute location identifies a place according to a standardized system of mathematical coordinates. Relative location, on the other hand, identifies a place in relation to some other place. For example, the absolute location of Chicago is 41° north and 87° west, while its location relative to Milwaukee, Wisconsin, would be 90 miles south on Interstate 94.

4. (A) Distribution refers to the spatial arrangement of items or features within a given area. For instance, a map indicating the location of each national park in the United States would demonstrate how these parks are spatially distributed throughout the country. Spatial arrangements of certain items or features can be described in terms of even or uneven distributions across space. In the case that many items are located close to one another, it is possible to say that these items are clustered together.

5. (E) A method for representing the three-dimensional surface of the earth on a two-dimensional map is known as projection. There are many different methods of map projection, including cylindrical, conical, and azimuthal projections. However, no single method of projection perfectly represents the three-dimensional surface of the earth.

6. (C) A subjective image of an area informed by individual perceptions and experiences in that area is known as a mental map. Unlike other kinds of maps, which are typically material representations shared by multiple users, mental maps are highly personal images about a place composed of subjective perceptions, memories, biases, and feelings.

7. **(B)** The notion that the physical environment offers certain constraints and opportunities that influence cultural practices without entirely determining them is known as possibilism. This idea stands contrary to the antiquated theory of environmental determinism, which posited that the physical environment absolutely determines how cultural practices develop in a given place. Possibilism, on the other hand, suggests that the physical environment offers certain possibilities that influence how a culture develops without absolutely determining this course of development.

8. **(A)** Culture is an abstract concept in human geography that broadly refers to human practices, beliefs, and behaviors that are specific to a place or region and that are created, shared, and/or altered over time. Cultures vary from place to place, converge and diverge over time, diffuse across space, and express human adaptations and innovations. Importantly, however, the transmission of culture is *not* biologically inherited. Rather, it is socially learned, or acquired.

9. **(C)** Globalization best illustrates the concept of cultural convergence because both ideas directly express processes in which diverse cultures become more similar and interrelated over time. Indeed, contemporary processes of globalization may be thought of as a modern-day instance of cultural convergence, in which the global diffusion of shared technologies and organizational structures is making different cultures more alike.

10. **(D)** The idea that material innovations, such as new technologies, diffuse more rapidly than newly exposed cultures can respond to them best illustrates the idea of cultural lag. Cultural lag describes this temporal delay between the arrival of a new innovation to a place and the ability of the local culture to adequately respond and adapt to this change. The arrival of a new technology to a place often poses significant cultural challenges, ranging from a lack of formal knowledge to potential ethical or religious conflicts that the new technology could create.

11. **(C)** The principle of distance decay describes a negative correlation between distance and degree of relation. Distance decay states that as the distance between two places *increases*, the intensity of relations between these places will *decrease*. For instance, distance decay theory assumes that a pair of towns 5 miles apart will have more in common than a pair of towns 500 miles apart. Therefore, the association between distance and degree of relation in distance decay theory is a negative correlation.

12. **(E)** The particular conditions that compel individuals or groups to migrate from one place to another are commonly referred to as push and pull factors. Push factors refer to the specific reasons that motivate an individual or group to leave a particular place. Pull factors, on the other hand, refer to the conditions in a new place that attract migrants to relocate to this place in particular.

13. (B) Economic and/or political associations that are comprised of multiple, autonomous member states that cooperate to achieve a common purpose are known as supranational organizations. Supranational means that the organization takes place at a level higher than the nation-state without threatening the autonomy, or independence, of each member nation-state. Some common examples of supranational organizations include the European Union (EU), the Caribbean Community (CARICOM), and the North American Free Trade Agreement (NAFTA).

14. (D) New Orleans is the city that describes a site along the Mississippi River and a situation as a primary port for offshore petroleum production in the Gulf of Mexico. While St. Louis and Minneapolis are cities sited along the Mississippi River, their situations are not as primary ports for offshore petroleum production, given their distance from the Gulf of Mexico. Alternatively, while Mobile and Houston are situated as ports for offshore petroleum production in the Gulf of Mexico, they are not sites along the Mississippi River.

15. (A) The ability to travel and communicate over greater distances in shorter amounts of time, due to technological innovations such as the airplane, automobile, telephone, and Internet, represents the idea of time-space compression. Time-space compression describes how new communication and transportation technologies, such as the examples above, radically alter the way humans experience time and space. Typically this experience is one in which time seems to accelerate and distance becomes a less formidable barrier.

16. (C) Latitude describes the location of a place in terms of its angular distance north or south of the equator. Like the rungs of a ladder, lines of latitude wrap horizontally around the earth and run parallel to the equator. Lines of latitude measure distances north and south of the equator, whereas lines of longitude measure distances east and west of the Prime Meridian.

17. (E) During the process of mapmaking, shape, area, distance, and direction are all liable to become distorted. Unfortunately, there is no absolutely perfect way to project the three-dimensional surface of the earth onto a flat, two-dimensional surface. With every projection, either shape, area, distance, direction, or a combination of these inevitably becomes distorted. However, the location of geographical features relative to one another should *not* be affected during the mapmaking process.

18. (A) The Prime Meridian, which passes through Greenwich, England, is equivalent to the line of 0° longitude. This location of the Prime Meridian is purely an arbitrary social convention, established among the scientific community in the late 19th century, in order to create a standardized system for determining the absolute location of things on the earth's surface.

19. (D) The geographical region whose center is located along the equator and whose area extends roughly 23° north and south of the equator is known as the tropical zone. This region, which wraps broadly around the equator, is also commonly referred to as the tropics or the torrid zone. The outer limits of this region are delimited by the Tropic of Capricorn in the Southern Hemisphere and the Tropic of Cancer in the Northern Hemisphere. It is not correct to call the tropics a rainforest region because rainforests are not exclusive to this region. Rather, rainforests extend well beyond the limits of the tropics. Rainforests that occur outside of the tropical zone are referred to as temperate rainforests.

20. (B) The term *scale* refers to a ratio between distances portrayed on a map and actual distances on the earth's surface that correspond to this map. To be useful, every map must include a scale that provides a corresponding ratio between distance on the map and actual distance on the earth's surface. An example of a map scale could be one inch on a map equals one mile on the actual surface of the earth.

21. (D) Processes of globalization, which result in the growth of global interconnections and interdependencies, are most closely associated with capitalism. Capitalism is a prevalent socioeconomic system that is characterized by private ownership, free enterprise, and profit motives. It is closely associated with globalization because capitalist expansion into new geographies of production and consumption are often cited as drivers behind the growth of global interconnections and interdependencies.

22. (E) A subfield of geography that deals holistically with the environmental and human attributes of a particular territory is known as regional geography. Regional geographers endeavor to understand how physical and cultural geographical features interrelate to form distinct regions, or spatial territories, whose attributes are uniquely different from other parts of the world. One example of a prominent regional approach would be Latin American geography.

23. (C) Remote sensing most directly refers to geographical techniques that collect information about the earth's surface from distantiated, or remote, perspectives. Remote sensing actually refers to a variety of techniques that capture data about the earth's surface from a distance. Remote-sensing techniques include satellite imagery and aerial photography, to cite two examples. While geographic information systems, or GIS, often incorporate data gathered through remote-sensing techniques, they encompass a broader range of tools and techniques than remote sensing alone.

24. (C) A hierarchy typically has strata in which social groups are ranked in a top to bottom fashion.

25. (A) In the context of the contemporary United States, a strip mall shopping center best exemplifies an ordinary landscape. Ordinary landscapes include scenes and spaces of daily life that individuals encounter on a regular basis and that often become a taken-for-granted aspect of their experience of the world.

26. (B) The forced dispersion of Jews from their ethnic homeland, which took place across many centuries, is a prominent example of diaspora. A diaspora describes the dispersion of an ethnic group from its homeland, typically as the result of direct or indirect outside forces that cause members of the group to relocate.

27. (C) The *site* of Mexico City is best described as a highland valley and dry lakebed located on a high plateau in southern central Mexico. While the remaining selections all accurately characterize Mexico City, they describe its situation rather than its site. Site refers to a place's local physical and environmental characteristics, while situation refers to a place's location relative to other places as well as its social significance in regional, national, or international contexts.

28. (D) Distance expressed in terms of the perceived amount of space separating one place from another best illustrates the concept of cognitive distance. Cognitive distance describes a highly subjective perception of distance that varies from person to person and from context to context. For instance, being able to pick up the phone to connect to someone living thousands of miles away tends to reduce the cognitive distance perceived to separate these two places.

29. (A) In cartography, parallels refer to lines of latitude. Lines of latitude, which encircle the earth along an east-west axis, are often referred to as parallels because they are perfectly parallel to one another. Unlike lines of longitude, which converge at the North and South Poles, lines of latitude never converge or intersect with one another.

30. (E) An impenetrable forest is least likely, among these selections, to be perceived as a path in cognitive space. Paths describe spatial passages or conduits that facilitate movement, rather than inhibiting it such as a thick, impenetrable forest would suggest. An impenetrable forest is more likely to be perceived as an edge, or boundary, in cognitive space.

31. (B) A vernacular region is one that does not have clearly defined borders; instead, it is an imprecise term used to describe large geographic areas such as the Deep South. Kansas, as a state with defined borders, is not a vernacular region.

32. (B) Thematic maps that employ a range of color tones to illustrate how particular values vary across predefined areas, such as counties, provinces, or states, are referred to as choropleth maps. A basic example would be a presidential election map of the United States in which each of the 50 states is colored either red or blue, according to which political party candidate received the majority of votes in each state.

33. (D) Curves on a topographic map that are used to illustrate specific values of elevation above or below sea level are known as contour lines. Topographical contours are typically irregularly shaped lines that connect points of equal elevation. Contour lines also illustrate the relative slope of elevation between various points. For instance, the slope between two points separated by 10 contour lines would be greater than the slope between two points separated by only 1 or 2 contour lines.

34. (B) Within the context of this data, 200 miles represents a critical distance. A critical distance is a threshold of distance beyond which the requisite travel costs or efforts are too great to make the journey viable or worthwhile for an individual or group.

35. (A) Map projections that preserve and accurately represent the *shape* of the geographical areas and features are said to be conformal.

36. (A) A cylindrical map projection would be most appropriate for producing a world map in which the equatorial zone is least distorted. In this example, the cylindrical surface is closest to the globe at its midregion, the earth's equator, where the globe is the greatest in circumference. Another way to state this relationship would be to say that the cylindrical projection is usually *tangent* to the earth's equator. Because cylindrical projections are typically tangent to the earth's equator, the middle latitudes are typically less distorted than the higher and lower latitudes in cylindrical projections.

37. (E) The cardinal points north, east, south, and west correspond to absolute direction. Their directions are absolute because they are based on physical astrological and geographical phenomena, such as the movement of the sun and the stars, which do not vary from place to place or culture to culture.

38. (D) Geomorphology, which is the study of landforms and landform processes, is the field of study that is *least associated* with human geography among the choices provided. Geomorphology is more closely aligned to physical geography. Human geography, on the other hand, is aligned with a variety of human-centered fields of study, including political science, anthropology, sociology, history, economics, cultural ecology, psychology, linguistics, religious studies, gender studies, urban planning, and demography.

39. (E) *Accessibility* and *connectivity* are two interrelated ways to describe spatial interactions between two or more objects distributed throughout space. Accessibility refers to the relative distance separating things in space, as well as the relative costs or difficulties inherent to accessing something in space. Connectivity refers to the quality of relations between two or more objects in space.

40. (B) Relative to lines of longitude near the equator, lines of longitude near the poles are closer together. This is the case because the overall circumference of the earth is smaller near the poles than at its center, near the equator.

41. (A) A network is a spatial domain of nodes, or places, that are integrated into a unified and functional system by a common set of linkages, routes, or connections.

(B) A network describes orderly flows of information, goods, or people that circulate between the various nodes in the system's domain. In this way it describes regular patterns of *mobility* between a set of determinate places. These patterns of movement describe how flows of information, goods, or people *diffuse* from place to place along preexisting routes or linkages that direct these flows in orderly and predictable directions. Also, because a network is defined as a functional system of nodes and linkages, or places and routes, it implies that each of these parts are *interdependent* on one another to keep flows of information, goods, or people circulating within the network. If one node or linkage breaks down, the entire flow of the network is also likely to become disrupted. Similarly, the network concept implies a system of relations between different places, so each is spatially *situated* in a unique position relative to the others. For instance, a place or node located closer to the middle of the network could be said to be more centrally located than a place or node located on the periphery.

(C) Networks are particularly relevant tools for describing spatial interactions in a globalized era because they are capable of representing complex, functional interrelationships and interdependencies among a growing number of places scattered across the globe. For instance, whereas all the parts for an automobile might have been manufactured in one factory 50 years ago, today the various parts of an automobile might be manufactured in dozens of different factories around the world. Given this complexity, a network diagram would be capable of demonstrating how an automobile's chain of production flows through many different factories in a globalized system of automobile manufacturing. Similarly, during a globalized era in which personal and professional social ties are becoming *more* distantiated and *less* place-based, virtual social networks provide an effective approach for understanding the spatial complexities of any particular individual's social linkages.

42. Many geographers theorize that a sense of placelessness is becoming a common way that people relate to their surroundings in modern, highly developed societies. While this theory is difficult to verify, there are many rationales to support it. First, with the rise of *industrialization*, it has become possible for attributes of place to become mass-produced in developed societies. For example, before industrialization in the United States, homes were individually crafted and built by hand so that no two were exactly alike. However, following industrialization, residential building components began to be mass-produced, resulting in the homogenization of home designs in the United States. This homogenization could support the idea of placelessness because it results in the dwindling uniqueness of certain features of places, like homes. Second, with the growth of mass communications, *popular cultures*, which exist across national and international scales, can be seen to be replacing *vernacular* or *folk cultures*, which previously existed across local and regional scales. As a result, the distinctiveness of different places has diminished as cultural tastes and preferences have become more popularized and mainstream. For instance, because of the widespread diffusion of mass communications such as the television, evidence suggests that local and regional dialects are becoming less common and standard dialects more common. This example could support the idea of placelessness because it suggests that one could travel to different regions of a developed society, such as the United States, and not get a sense of the distinctions that previously gave different places and regions a unique sense of identity. Third, with processes of *globalization*, places spread out across the globe generally are becoming more interdependent and interrelated socioeconomically. As a result of globalization, it is now possible to travel to different world cities and find the same transnational corporate enterprises such as restaurants, retail stores, banks, and hotels. This contributes to a sense of placelessness because one can conceivably be in Tokyo or New York and frequent the same corporate establishments, which, from the inside, are virtually indistinguishable. Finally, with an increase in *mobility* in highly developed societies, people are less rooted to particular places than in the past. For instance, whereas 100 years ago the average person spent his or her entire life in one place, nowadays it is not uncommon for the average person to relocate several times throughout his or her lifetime. This general increase in mobility has arguably weakened the strong attachments to home and an attendant sense of place. In general these four developments of industrialization, widespread popular cultures, globalization, and an increase in mobility may all be used to support the theory that a sense of placelessness is becoming a more common way that people relate to their surroundings in highly developed, modern societies.

Chapter 2: Population

43. (C) Nigeria is a country experiencing rapid population growth and has a high percentage of young people approaching or at child-bearing age. The population pyramid with a wide base reflects the high percentage of young people. Japan, Germany, and Russia are all experiencing zero population growth, which would result in a narrow base on the population pyramid. The United States is experiencing slow population growth resulting in a slightly larger base that remains relatively constant throughout the ages until slightly decreasing at the top of the pyramid.

44. (C) According to the four stages of the demographic transition model, as countries industrialize, birth and death rates decrease over time due to increased access to health care, education (particularly among women), and other social changes.

45. (D) The first stage of the demographic transition model indicates that total population is low and constant due to high birth and death rates. This is common in preindustrial societies where women have many children that help support the household. Population does not increase since death rates remain high due to lack of medical care.

46. (B) Stage four of the demographic transition model experiences low birth rates since women are being educated and economies are not dependent on child labor. Subsistence agriculture requires children to work family farms and therefore would actually encourage high birth rates. Increased sanitation and availability of health care would have greater impacts on death rates than birth rates.

47. (D) Moral restraint is the only example of a preventive check. Disease, war, famine, and disasters are examples of positive checks. In general, preventive checks result in lower birth rates, while positive checks result in higher death rates.

48. (A) Malthus believed that only the upper class could enforce moral restraint to limit family size. Additionally, he argued that wealthy families should limit their family size to prevent dividing up their wealth among many heirs. Malthus felt that money should not be taken away from the moral upper class to help the unmoral lower class. He discouraged programs that would help the lower class and actually encouraged poor health habits and poor living conditions among the lower class to reduce the population.

49. (D) India contains three megacities: New Delhi, Mumbai, and Kolkata. A megacity has a population greater than 15 million. The other countries each contain one megacity: São Paulo, Brazil; New York City, United States; Shanghai, China; and Mexico City, Mexico.

50. (C) Optimum population theory suggests that there is an optimal size for a population based on resource availability and carrying capacity. China instituted its one-child policy to limit population growth to reach an optimal level. The other choices are not real theories.

51. (B) A low unemployment rate is not a result of overpopulation, while insufficient housing, overcrowding, deforestation, and lack of resources are all consequences.

52. (A) Sub-Saharan Africa has the largest rate of natural increase (RNI) due to high birth rates. The RNI is the crude birth rate minus the crude death rate. North America, Australia, Russian Domain, and Europe all have neutral or negative RNI due to low birth rates.

53. (E) Arithmetic population density is a measure of population per unit area and therefore equals the total population divided by the total land area.

54. (A) Loss of tax base and increased poverty are two examples of problems city centers faced following suburbanization in the 1960s. Only in the past decade have city centers attempted to renovate to try to attract people back downtown. Gentrification is the process of turning lower-income neighborhoods into more expensive areas for the upper class. As people moved to the suburbs, many businesses and jobs also relocated out of the city center. The increased popularity of personal cars helped spur suburbanization as the need for public transportation decreased.

55. (D) Commercial farming and the increased use of machinery to replace human labor resulted in rural population decline in the United States and Canada in the 1900s. Urban decentralization is the migration of people from city centers to the suburbs. The growth of the Sunbelt began in the 1970s as a result of an expanding Southern economy and the low cost of living. The warm weather and availability of air-conditioning were also attractive to Northerners. Counterurbanization is a trend in which people migrate from large cities to small towns for the lower cost of living and job opportunities. The "black exodus" from the South refers to African American populations that migrated from the southern United States to the North and West during the early 20th century because of job availability.

56. (B) Urban primacy is when a country has a primary city that is three or four times larger than any other city in the country. It is common in Latin America and can be a problem since so many natural resources are concentrated in one urban area.

57. (D) Developed countries such as the United States, Australia, and France have a lower rate of natural increase than less developed countries such as Honduras, Bangladesh, and Chad. Rate of natural increase is the crude birth rate minus the crude death rate of a population. Developing countries have higher crude birth rates, crude death rates, and fertility rates than developed countries.

58. (A) During the 1990s, the United States experienced high levels of immigration (people moving to the United States), which contributed to slow population increase. The birth, fertility, and death rates did not change substantially during this decade. Emigration, when people leave their home country to move elsewhere, was also low during this decade.

59. (D) A limiting factor is something that limits population growth. Food, water, and living space are all examples of limiting factors. Without access to these resources, populations cannot grow and eventually decline. The other choices are not real factors.

60. (B) Carrying capacity is the maximum population size that an environment can support. In general, populations increase when they are below the carrying capacity because there are plenty of resources available for the entire population. However, populations decrease when they are above carrying capacity because resources are not available for everyone.

61. (C) Measuring the doubling time of a population requires that the growth rate be constant over long periods of time.

62. (D) In the United States women had fewer children in 1995 than in 1955, which is the baby boom era. Also, women are having children later in life; there is a clear shift from women having children in their early twenties in 1955 to women having children in their early thirties in 1995.

63. (A) A push factor is any circumstance or event that would make someone want to leave his or her home country and migrate elsewhere. Examples include war, famine, disasters, and lack of jobs. Pull factors are the reasons immigrants want to settle in a new country, such as religious freedom or job opportunity.

64. (C) A baby boom is a sharp population increase that reflects a period of peace and prosperity. In general, fertility rates decrease when women seek higher levels of education and competitive jobs. Following World War II, the United States experienced a baby boom between 1946 and 1964.

65. (B) Demographic data describes the characteristics of a population. For example, the U.S. Census collects demographic data such as age, gender, race, and income.

66. (D) The dependency ratio is the number of people between 14 and 64 years of age (working age) compared to the number of people aged 65 or older (retirement age) and under 14 years old (children) in a population. A high dependency ratio suggests that many people in the population are classified as dependent, under the age of 14 and over the age of 65.

67. (E) Since women have longer life expectancies than men, the majority of older persons in developed countries are women. Since women tend to outlive men, they are often single in older age while men tend to remarry. In developed countries, the older populations are growing at significantly faster rates than the younger population as a result of low birth and death rates. In the 2000 and 2004 elections the 60–70 age group had higher voter turnout rates than any other age group.

68. (A) Zimbabwe has the lowest life expectancy at birth, 49.64 years for the total population. Japan, Chile, Switzerland, and Canada all have life expectancies at birth of 75 years or more.

69. (D) *Remittance* is the term for when a migrant sends money back to family still living in his or her home country. It is considered a form of international aid.

70. (B) A cohort is a group of people that share characteristics or experiences. In population geography, a cohort is any group of individuals that is from the same generation.

71. (C) A temporary increase in births is called a baby boom, such as the one that occurred after World War II.

72. (E) Demographic momentum describes a population that, because of the high percentage of people of child-bearing age, continues to grow after fertility rates decline.

73. (D) A contagious disease, such as influenza, is passed through a population from contact with an infected person. In hierarchical diffusion, the disease spreads from high-density urban areas to rural areas. Network diffusion occurs along transportation and/or social networks, and relocation diffusion occurs when the disease migrates to new regions. Mixed diffusion is a combination of the other types of diffusion.

74. (B) Ecumene is the proportion of land that is occupied by permanent human settlement (the built environment) compared to the amount of undeveloped land.

75. (A) Neo-Malthusians incorporate the rapid growth of developing countries into their overpopulation theory as well as examine the lack of other resources such as sanitation and medicine for the survival of people. Malthus mainly focused on the availability of food as the limiting factor of population growth. Neither neo-Malthusians nor Malthusians believe that technological advances can help sustain a population by producing required resources.

76. (E) Cyclic movement is a type of migration that has a clear cycle, such as a nomadic tribe that moves to specific locations each season based on food availability.

77. (C) The gravity model uses the size and distance of two cities to determine how people and services will move between them. Larger cities that are closer together will have a higher exchange rate of people, ideas, and goods than smaller cities that are farther apart.

78. (D) Transhumance is defined as the seasonal movement of livestock between pasture areas in the lowlands and mountains with a focus on vertical movement by changing elevation. Step migration is a series of small moves from relatively similar places to more different areas; for example, moving from a rural area to a small town to a city. Transmigration is a mass move of people from one place to another, such as to alleviate overcrowding. Periodic movement is a type of relocation that is temporary, such as military service or college. Finally, interregional migration is a permanent movement from one area of a country to another.

79. (A) Chain migration is when one family member migrates to a new country where he or she earns money to help the rest of the family move to that country at a later date. It is very common among families migrating from Mexico to the United States.

80. (B) In the United States, fertility rates are highest among low-income groups. Fertility rates are also higher in rural areas when compared to metropolitan areas and among women with high school degrees when compared to college graduates. The United States has also experienced a trend of women having children later in life. Finally, certain ethnicities such as Hispanics and African Americans tend to have higher fertility rates than other groups, such as whites.

81. (C) Developing countries have tried to make land that is already farmed more productive by using genetically modified plants that are more productive and can require less water, pesticides, and chemical fertilizers. Often new farmland is unavailable, so farmers must find ways to increase productivity of already established farms. The use of genetically modified crops has increased in these countries, resulting in higher crop yields.

82. (C) The Middle East and North Africa have the lowest per capita freshwater resources (760 cubic meters), while Latin America and Asia enjoy the largest freshwater resource (10,000 or more cubic meters).

83. (E) China has only 0.111 hectares per person of arable land. Kazakhstan (1.513 hectares), Canada (1.444 hectares), Australia (2.395 hectares), and Argentina (0.734 hectares) enjoy greater availability of farmland. In general the temperate and continental climates have more arable land; Europe and Central Asia have the highest amount of arable land available per capita.

84. (B) Gerrymandering is used to manipulate voting districts to impact future elections. Areas that have a stable voting pattern over time are most susceptible to gerrymandering. Packing is a strategy used in gerrymandering where the opposition party is packed into one district to increase the party's power in the other districts. Reapportionment is when the size of state congressional delegations are redefined due to new census information. *Riding* is the Canadian term for an electoral district. *Repositioning* is not a term used in political geography.

85. (C) Spatial patterns of populations are described as uniform, random, or clustered. The Homestead Act of 1862 allocated rectangular parcels of land comprising

160 acres each. This resulted in a uniform pattern of rural population distribution that is evident today.

86. (E) Environmental resistance is the difference between the actual growth of a population and its potential growth that is limited by factors including competition, food availability, climate, and predators.

87. (D) Fecundity is the maximum potential of a population to reproduce. Sterility is the inability to produce children. The terms *fruitful*, *prolific*, and *fertility* refer to the ability to produce children.

88. (B) A dispersed population distribution is when a population is evenly distributed across an area. This is especially common in rural farming areas. The opposite is concentrated distribution, in which people are densely grouped in an urban area.

89. (A) The gross national product (GNP) is the amount of goods and services produced by a country in one year divided by the number of people living in the country.

90. (A) A guest worker is someone who leaves his or her country to work in another country without the intent to settle permanently. Typically, the labor is physical, and young people are best suited for the work.

91. (C) The rule of 70 is an approximation of the doubling time for a population. For any population growing at a constant rate, divide 70 by the annual growth rate to determine the approximate amount of time it will take for the population to double.

92. (B) A choropleth map uses different colors to represent varying quantities in defined areas, such as states or countries. The quantities can represent percentages, densities, or rates. A cartogram is a map with distorted area and shape to emphasize a thematic variable, such as the GNP or HIV-infection rates. A flow line map uses arrows to indicate the flow or transfer of goods, services, or people. A dot map uses dots to represent a distribution of goods, people, or services. An isoline map uses isolines to connect areas with the same values and is common in representing not only population but also climate and agriculture.

93. (E) Malaria is endemic to tropical or subtropical regions. An endemic disease is continuously present within the population of a region. An epidemic is a disease, like the plague, that affects many people for a period of time then subsides. A pandemic is a widespread epidemic that could affect large areas such as continents or even the entire world. A prosodemic is a disease that is transferred directly from one person to another. Endodermic refers to a layer of cells in an embryo.

94. (D) Standard of living indicates the wealth and material goods available to each person in a country. Developed countries enjoy higher standards of living than developing countries; therefore, standard of living can indicate the level of development of a country.

95. (A) A J-curve suggests that population projections indicate exponential growth. The population line mimics the shape of the letter *J*, where population growth is initially slow and then increases dramatically.

96. (C) Most developed countries (MDC) have higher literacy rates than least developed countries (LDC). Literacy is defined as the ability to read and write. LDC are categorized by the United Nations based on socioeconomic factors such as gross national income, health, education, nutrition, and economic vulnerability.

97. (B) An intervening opportunity is an environmental or cultural factor that encourages migration.

98. (E) Core countries are developed, produce new innovations, and serve as a central place for trade. The United States is an example of a core country.

99. (A) A periphery country is generally less developed and a poorer nation. Periphery countries are not central in the trade of goods and services or development of new innovations.

100. (D) According to Ravenstein's migration laws, most international migrants are young males, while women are more likely to migrate within their own country.

101. (E) A country enters Stage Five of the Demographic Transition Model when the birth rate declines until it is lower than the death rate. However, other demographic factors can prevent overall negative population growth.

102. (C) A forced migration is the result of religious or political persecution, war, natural disasters, forced labor, or famine. The California gold rush was not a forced migration, as people moved to the American West looking for gold and new opportunity.

103. (C) A brain drain is when highly educated, intelligent, or professional people choose to migrate in large numbers, either for better pay or living conditions in other countries or to escape turmoil in their home country.

104. (B) Emigration, the process of leaving one's home country to settle in another place, can reduce the pressure on land in overpopulated areas.

105. (A) Harvesting plants twice a year is known as double cropping. It can result in poor soil quality and can lead to migration.

106. (C) A type of rural settlement with several families living close together and surrounded by farms is known as nucleated.

107. (D) A refugee is a person who is forced to leave his or her homeland because of persecution, or fear of persecution due to their race, religion, nationality, political opinion, or social status; war; or other violence. Following WWII many refugees left Eastern Europe because of persecution and violence.

108. (B) A consequence of negative population growth is reduced strain on resources, including land, food, and water.

109. (A) When countries practice female infanticide, or the deliberate killing of girl babies, the end result can be an unbalanced sex ratio where there are substantially more people of one sex than the other.

110. (D) While all of the other choices either reduce the fecundity (fertility) rates of the female population of a developed country or reduce the number of children per household, choice (D), immigration rate, is not factored into the calculation for RNI.

111. (C) Because TFR is simply the number of live births divided by the number of women of birthing age, and because neither of these numbers can be below zero for any population, TFR cannot be negative.

112. (E) Countries in stage one tend to be pre-industrial, agricultural societies with high birth and death rates as well as high rates of infant mortality and a focus on large families to provide farm labor. No modern countries are currently in this stage of demographic transition, however, most societies would have been considered in this stage prior to the 18th century.

113. (B) Neo-Malthusians, who subscribe to some of the population theories advanced in the 19th century by Thomas Malthus, believe that resource consumption and increasing demand will present significant issues for the global community as world population increases in the coming decades.

114. (D) Brownsville, in southern Texas, is very close to the Mexican border. As such, the population graph for Brownsville very closely resembles that of Mexico. None of the other factors mentioned would result in a triangle-shaped graph.

115. (A) Voluntary movement to a series of more and more economically advantageous locations is a type of step migration.

116. (B) The high cost of land is considered a push factor. All of the other choices are factors that might entice people to immigrate to another country.

117. (C) The population center of the United States has moved westward in every census since 1790, and in recent years it has moved slightly southward as well, so that it is now located in the south central part of Missouri.

118. (E) Countries like Uzbekistan and Iraq have high physiologic densities but not high arithmetic densities.

119. (B) As populations of developed countries age, the prevalence of chronic diseases has increased, placing an increased burden on the health-care systems of those countries.

120. (D) According to Thomas Malthus, populations of poor people could not be controlled exclusively by preventive checks. Malthus advocated cutting off charitable aid to the poor and increasing the likelihood that positive checks such as disease would take over to control the surplus population of poor people. In the Malthusian model, a large surplus population of poor people was a hindrance to economic activity and social development, not an integral part of it.

121. (A) The epidemiological transition model suggests that the cause of death changes in a society from communicative diseases to degenerative diseases over time. The model is divided into three stages. The first stage experiences high and fluctuating mortality rates due to epidemic diseases and famine. Life expectancy at birth is low during this stage at approximately 30 years. The second stage experiences less frequent pandemics, and as a result mortality rates decline. Life expectancy during the second stage increases to around 50 years. Additionally, population growth begins to increase exponentially. The third stage is when mortality is mostly caused by degenerative and man-made diseases, such as high blood pressure, lung cancer, and cardiovascular disease. In this stage, mortality rates continue to decline until reaching low stable levels. Average life expectancy increases to 70 years or more. At this stage, fertility and birth rates are the major factor in population growth, which is stable and either slowly increasing or even decreasing.

(B) Longer life expectancies at birth can be attributed to many factors, including better access to health care, improved nutrition, and increased sanitation. Decreased exposure to environmental pollution can also contribute to longer life expectancies.

122. Stouffer's law of intervening opportunities suggests that migration to a new location is directly proportional to the opportunities at the destination. Therefore, the place of departure has fewer opportunities than the destination. Intervening opportunities are factors that persuade a migrant to settle en route instead of continuing to the original destination. Intervening opportunities offer opportunities complementary to the ones originally sought at the planned destination, such as jobs, land, education, and political or religious freedom. Additionally, intervening obstacles could result in settlement en route because of language barriers, international boundaries, or anxieties about the planned destination.

Push and pull factors can be physical, demographic, economic, social, or political. Push factors are reasons to leave a homeland and migrate elsewhere. Some examples of push factors include natural disasters, famine, lack of work, overcrowding, war, and political instability. Pull factors are reasons to migrate to a new location; examples include labor demand, higher wages, religious freedom, better living conditions, education opportunities, and political stability. Pull factors are not always real and can be imaginary reasons, such as the rumors that American streets were paved with gold to entice new immigrants from Europe during the 19th century.

Chapter 3: Culture

123. (C) Kazakhstan's dominant native language, Kazakh, belongs to the Uralic language family. Dominant native languages in Libya, Cambodia, and Portugal and Germany belong, respectively, to the Afro-Asiatic, Sino-Tibetan, and Indo-European language families.

124. (E) An isogloss is a geographical boundary that indicates the outer limit of one particular linguistic feature, such as a word's pronunciation, spelling, or meaning. Unlike language borders, isoglosses indicate linguistic differences that can occur both within and between language regions.

125. (B) Ayers Rock, located in Australia, is the only selection associated with a traditional, or tribal, religion in which the local natural formations are regarded as embodying, rather than symbolizing, spiritual beings.

126. (A) Because of the historical geography of the United States' migration and settlement patterns, which generally began along the Atlantic seaboard and radiated westward over time, cultural diffusions have likewise tended to flow from east to west over much of the country's history.

127. (D) The relative isolation of a Hindu temple located in Texas, far from its religious hearth in India, would most likely indicate relocation diffusion as a result of migration from India to Texas.

128. (E) Ahimsa is a religious tenet shared by Hinduism and Buddhism. The only region among the choices that fully corresponds to either of these faiths is the Indian subcontinent, which is a predominantly Hindu region.

129. (C) Chain migration, residential segregation, multiculturalism, and multinucleated urban structure all support the notion that ethnic enclaves should persist for one reason or another. Structural assimilation, on the other hand, measures the ability of a minority group to fully integrate into the host society, a process that necessarily undermines the integrity of ethnic enclaves.

130. (D) The adobe house is ideally suited for a diurnal climate characterized by hot daytime temperatures and cold nighttime temperatures because its thick earthen walls absorb heat in the day and release it at night. This is why adobe is a vernacular architectural style common to the American Southwest, where a diurnal climate is present.

131. (B) Folk cultures are more homogeneous than popular cultures because they belong to smaller groups of individuals who share a common local environment, a common history, and common values. Unlike popular cultures, folk cultures are more insulated, less exposed to outside influences, and less liable to frequent changes over time.

132. (B) By process of elimination, a dialect can be neither a *language branch*, *language group*, nor *language family*, given that these terms describe collections of multiple languages and a dialect is a trait of only one language. Similarly, a dialect cannot be a cultural complex because the latter refers to a collection of multiple cultural traits. Therefore, a dialect must represent a cultural trait, a single aspect of an overarching cultural complex.

133. (A) A Mormon church located in a rural area of northwestern Colorado is most likely the result of expansion diffusion, given the proximity of northwestern Colorado to the Mormon religious hearth, located in the neighboring state of Utah.

134. (D) A built landscape that shows evidence of abandonment, disinvestment, and general neglect is considered derelict. Derelict landscapes can range from vacant housing complexes in disrepair to abandoned factories to littered and overgrown recreational fields, to name a few examples.

135. (E) Genocide, also called ethnic cleansing, is the deliberate killing of a large group of people, especially those of a particular ethnic group or nationality.

136. (B) In the core-domain-sphere model developed by Donald Melnig, the core is the cultural center of a particular region, where most of the cultural traits are widespread.

137. (B) A trend or innovation that diffuses to major nodes before diffusing to smaller nodes, regardless of their distances in relation to the point of origin, is an example of hierarchical diffusion. Unlike expansion diffusion, which spreads uniformly through space, hierarchical diffusion spreads nonuniformly through space.

In this case, for instance, a new fashion trend diffuses to other world cities more quickly than it does to less urbanized areas, even though the latter is closer in distance to the point of origin than the former. The answer is not relocation diffusion because a fashion trend does not migrate, but rather spreads hierarchically while also remaining in place at the point of origin.

138. (C) Vernacular culture regions are informal regions based on popular perceptions or feelings about an area. Unlike formal culture regions, vernacular cultural regions are *not* defined according to the presence of specific cultural traits. Unlike functional culture regions, which may be objectively measured and defined, vernacular cultural regions characteristically lack proper boundaries and determinate organizational features. Another common example of a vernacular culture region in the United States is Dixie.

139. (A) An immigrant who selectively adopts only certain customs of the dominant host society while retaining much of his or her native culture is an example of acculturation. Unlike assimilation, which implies a process that culminates in the full adoption of the dominant host society's customs, acculturation implies a more selective and less complete process of adjustment in which one's native culture does not become fully displaced by the host culture.

140. (B) Pidgin is a highly simplified language created among linguistically diverse groups in order to facilitate basic communications between these groups. By definition, pidgin is not the first language of any of its speakers, as its express purpose is to facilitate communication between speakers whose native tongues are dissimilar. Once a pidgin language develops into a native language for a certain group of speakers, it becomes a Creole language.

141. (D) Mandarin, the official language of the People's Republic of China, is the only language among these choices that does not belong to the Indo-European language family. Mandarin belongs to the Sino-Tibetan language family. Hindi, Bengali, Farsi, and Dutch, which are primarily spoken in India, Iran, and northern Europe, all belong to the Indo-European language family, which also includes Romanic and Germanic languages such as Spanish, French, German, and English.

142. (E) A minaret is a slender, vertical tower common to mosques, or Islamic houses of worship. In addition to possessing symbolic value as a marker of Islam on the landscape, minarets also serve a practical function as an elevated platform from which calls for prayer are broadcast to the surrounding area several times a day.

143. (C) San Jose is the toponym, or place name, that best belongs in a formal culture region defined by shared traits of Spanish language and Catholicism. While Saint Paul qualifies as a Catholic toponym, it is not properly a Spanish toponym.

144. (C) Kashmir, a region that occupies parts of northern India, eastern Pakistan, and western China, is characterized as a zone of conflict between the Muslim and Hindu ethnic groups of Pakistan and India, respectively. During the latter half of the 20th century several wars were fought between Pakistan and India for control of this disputed territory. Chechnya, Kurdistan, East Timor, and the West Bank are also zones of ethnic-religious conflict. However, the first three areas of conflict are primarily between Muslim and Christian ethnic groups, while the latter is between Muslim and Jewish ethnic groups.

145. (E) A secular landscape is one that does *not* have explicit associations to any particular religion. The only iconic landscape among the choices that is not explicitly secular is Dome of the Rock, a religious mosque in Jerusalem that represents an important symbol of Islam.

146. (D) A discrete territorial unit whose borders are situated entirely within a larger territorial unit is considered an enclave. In this instance, Lesotho is an enclave state situated within the territorial borders of the Republic of South Africa.

147. (B) Christianity is best associated with proselytism, which is a practice that actively encourages religious conversion. Whereas religious conversion is actively promoted in many Christian denominations, proselytism is not traditionally practiced in the other religions listed.

148. (A) Sharia law is an Islamic code of conduct that regulates personal conduct and social affairs in a particular territory. It is enforced, to varying degrees, in Islamic states such as Saudi Arabia, Iran, Yemen, and Somalia, to name a few. Turkey, despite a majority Muslim population, has a secular government and does not subscribe to Sharia law.

149. (E) A lingua franca is an established language adopted by speakers in a particular place or context in order to facilitate communication among a linguistically diverse group. It is typically a second language shared by a group of speakers whose native tongues are mutually unintelligible. Unlike pidgin, which is a primitive language created for the purpose of communication between linguistically diverse speakers, a lingua franca is an already developed language that is adopted by speakers as a second language.

150. (B) The successive Islamic and Christian influences evident in the cultural landscape of the Alhambra illustrate the concept of sequent occupance. Sequent occupance describes how later stages of cultural modification in a place are influenced by earlier modifications made by their predecessors in such a way that a distinctive cultural imprint sediments over time.

151. (C) A spatial system organized around one or more hubs, nodes, or focal points, whose domain of influence exhibits identifiable areas of core and periphery, represents a functional culture region. Communication and transportation networks are prime examples of functional culture regions.

152. (A) A holistic approach to studying the relationship between a human society and its natural environment is known as cultural ecology. Cultural ecologists endeavor to understand how humans and natural environments relate to one another to produce unified systems of flows, influences, interactions, and outcomes, much like an ecosystem.

153. (D) A significant imbalance in the ratio of males to females in population cohorts under the age of 30 in China, a result of the country's one-child policy, could be cited as evidence of all the selections *except* gender longevity gap. Gender longevity gap describes the statistical difference between the average life expectancies of women and men. This could account for a significant gender imbalance in older age cohorts of a population; however, it should not significantly affect younger age cohorts. Rather, the underrepresentation of women in these age cohorts represents a maladaptive reaction to the state's authoritarian one-child policy shaped by a culture of gender discrimination and practices of female infanticide.

154. (B) A prohibition that forbids Hindus to slaughter or consume beef is an example of a religious proscription. Religious proscriptions are specific rules that ban certain practices among a religion's followers. It is not uncommon for religions to proscribe the consumption of certain foods, such as the proscription against consuming pork for Muslims and Jews.

155. (E) Hinduism, Jainism, Sikhism, and Buddhism are all religions that originated in the Indian subcontinent, south of the Himalayas. Zoroastrianism, on the other hand, originated northwest of the Indian subcontinent, in Persia, or present-day Iran.

156. (A) Two prominent French ethnic islands, or areas of French ethnic concentration, in North America are historically located in Louisiana and Quebec. Both of these regions were colonized by French emigrants beginning in the late 17th century, before the formation of the United States and Canada.

157. (D) The term *white flight* describes a residential exodus of primarily white, middle- and upper-class residents from multiethnic urban areas to ethnically homogeneous suburban and exurban areas during the second half of the 20th century in the United States. White flight is associated with the growth of suburban and exurban areas, the persistence of de facto racial segregation, residential discriminatory practices, and socioeconomic practices that shifted wealth and investments outside of urban centers, leading to their blight and decay. However, white flight is *not* associated with processes of gentrification, which represent reinvestments and redevelopments in urban centers and which generally followed the era of white flight in the United States.

158. (E) Zionism is a Jewish claim to Palestine as their rightful national homeland. It is primarily a widespread political movement, founded in religious doctrine, which advocates the sovereignty of Israel as the territorial state for the Jewish nation.

159. (B) Arabic, which spread westward into northern Africa with the diffusion of Islam, is part of the Afro-Asiatic language family. The Afro-Asiatic language family spans most of northern Africa and the Arabian Peninsula, from the Atlantic Ocean to the Arabian Sea.

160. (C) The word *taboo* refers to a restriction on behavior that comes from social customs, such as eating pork in some cultures, or wearing certain types of clothing.

161. (B) Judaism, which is based on the belief in one God, is characterized as a monotheistic religion. Judaism is one of the three major monotheistic religions in the world, along with Christianity and Islam.

162. (D) The belief that one's own culture is inherently superior is a key concept of ethnocentrism. In human geography, ethnocentrism describes the erroneous belief that the entire world operates, or should operate, according to the customs and values of one's own culture. However, in reality, different cultures have different customs, beliefs, and practices, which cannot be properly understood according to only one cultural template.

163. (B) The Ganges River is a sacred place whose waters possess special religious significance for Hindus. Among the choices, the Ganges River, which flows through much of northern India, is the only selection whose geography corresponds to the Hindu culture region.

164. (D) Polytheism is not a cultural trait common to Muslim regions of the world where Islamic religious traditions are predominant. Islam is a monotheistic religion, meaning that its followers believe in only one god rather than multiple gods. Fasting, pilgrimage, Sharia law, and daily ritual prayers are all cultural traits common to Islam.

165. (B) Because constructed languages like Esperanto contain elements of existing languages, they cannot by definition be considered language isolates. All the other statements are true of language isolates.

166. (A) A reconstructed language from which a number of related modern languages all derive is known as a protolanguage. A protolanguage can be thought of as a common ancestral tongue for a particular language branch, or subfamily. In the case of the Romance language subfamily, Latin is the common ancestral language, or protolanguage.

167. (D) The English language properly belongs to the Germanic language branch of the Indo-European language family. While certain words in the modern English language derive from non-Germanic language branches, the overall structure of the language belongs to the Germanic language branch.

168. (C) In Islam the religious practice of "sacred struggle" is known as jihad. Although jihad has recently acquired negative connotations to Islamic fundamentalism and terrorism in the West, it is generally regarded among Muslims as a broader term to signify any act of religious struggle, whether violent or peaceful.

169. (E) The concept of nirvana is most closely associated with Buddhism, among the choices offered. The concept, however, is not exclusive to the Buddhist religion. It is also an important concept to several other Indian religions, including Hinduism and Jainism. Generally, nirvana signifies a peaceful state of mind and body that is free of suffering or want.

170. (A) In Chad one is most likely to encounter speakers whose native tongue belongs to the Nilo-Saharan language family. This language family, which roughly corresponds to the Sahara desert region of north-central Africa, represents a group of languages that are mainly spoken in Chad but also in neighboring Niger, Nigeria, and Cameroon.

171. (C) The Mayan language corresponds to the Yucatan Peninsula of Mexico. Of the selections provided, Mayan is the only Amerindian language proper to the territory now known as Mexico.

172. (D) The concept that refers to a group of people who all speak the same language is known as a speech community. The terms *language family* and *language group*, on the other hand, refer to collections of languages rather than speakers.

173. (C) Ireland was the site of violent religious conflicts between Catholic and Protestant Christian groups throughout much of the 20th century. Specifically, this violent conflict took place primarily in Northern Ireland, a contentious region in which Catholics and Protestants live in proximity to one another and have long battled for political control of this disputed territory.

174. (E) The term that characterizes a social decline in religious adherence is *secularism*. Generally, secularism is thought to be correlated to a host of social transformations that take place as a particular society industrializes. Among many industrialized European nations, for instance, a marked decline in religious adherence has been observed relative to preindustrial levels of religious affiliation.

175. (C) The Upper Midwest region of the United States has the strongest historical connections to Lutheran Christian traditions. Traditionally, New England has strong ties to Catholicism, the South has strong ties to Baptist traditions, and the Rocky Mountains have strong ties to the Church of the Latter-Day Saints, or the Mormon church. The Pacific Northwest is generally regarded as a culture region with no distinct religious affiliation.

176. (B) The term *caste* refers to a particular system of social stratification that is informed by Hindu religious beliefs. As such, the caste system of social stratification is a prominent trait of traditional folk culture in India. The caste system assigns each individual to a specific social position that affords a prescribed set of rights, duties, and obligations for that person.

177. (A) Shinto, a set of rituals and customs that are practiced in order to connect with ancient spirits, is a religious tradition that belongs to the nation of Japan. Shinto is a religious tradition that is indigenous to Japan yet also greatly influenced by Buddhist beliefs, which later diffused into Japan. As such, Shinto may be regarded as a religion with both traditional and syncretic attributes.

178. (D) The Balkan Peninsula describes a conflict region between various ethnic groups, including Serbs, Albanians, and Bosnians. The Balkan Peninsula is located in southeastern Europe and is comprised of countries such as Greece, Montenegro, Macedonia, Bulgaria, Serbia, and Bosnia and Herzegovina. Historically a region of ethnic heterogeneity and conflict, it is often referred to vernacularly as the "powder keg."

179. (E) The largest branch of Islam, to which as many as 80 percent of all Muslims belong, is called Sunni Islam. The Sunni branch of Islam is predominant across northern Africa, the Arabian Peninsula, and much of southwestern Asia. Meanwhile, the smaller branch of Islam, Shia Islam, is predominant in Iran, but also in parts of Iraq, Turkey, Afghanistan, and Pakistan. This religious divide between Sunnis and Shias is often the source of ethnic conflict in the Middle East.

180. (D) The distance between groups that comes about because of social issues such as race, class, ethnicity, and sexuality is called social distance.

181. (D) A small religious group that is an offshoot of a larger religion is called a sect.

182. (E) Bluegrass gospel songs are not an example of material culture in North America, because songs are not properly material objects, or artifacts. Instead, things like songs and stories are nonmaterial *ideas* that express the values, histories, and beliefs of a particular culture.

183. (D) Given this information, the Canadian province of Quebec is most likely to feature the Norman cottage because Quebec is a North American region in which a great number of French immigrants settled. Indeed, the Norman cottage is prevalent throughout Quebec as a product of relocation diffusion.

184. (C) The Nebraskan city of Lincoln best belongs in a vernacular culture region called the Corn Belt. Nebraska is located in a temperate grassland region classified as prairie, which covers much of the Great Plains region of the United States. This region is often referred to as the Corn Belt or Grain Belt because of the large quantities of agricultural grains produced there.

185. (A) The toponyms *Leninskoye* and *Stalinsk* are found in Russia. These place names refer to Vladimir Lenin and Joseph Stalin, respectively. Lenin and Stalin were two leaders of the former Soviet Union, which included Russia.

186. (C) A revived language is a written or spoken language that has nearly died out but then has experienced a resurgence due to the active interest of a community and has regained some of its former status and importance. Examples of revived languages include Hawaiian, Hebrew, Sanscrit, and several Native American languages such as Wampanoag.

187. (A) A religion that is characterized by a set of beliefs and rituals that are tied to a specific group of people or place and primarily passed down through generations is an *ethnic* religion, in contrast to a universalizing religion which actively seeks new converts.

188. (D) In the context of Papua New Guinea's geography of language, mountains and islands represent barriers to diffusion. Barriers to diffusion are social characteristics and/or geographical features that prevent the spread of cultural innovations and preserve the unique cultural attributes of local places.

189. (E) The place or area where a cultural practice originates is known as a hearth. A hearth can be thought of as a home or cradle for new ideas, beliefs, and innovations. For instance, the place where a particular religion originates is called a religious hearth.

190. (C) The two largest language families in the world, in terms of absolute numbers of speakers, are Sino-Tibetan and Indo-European. Together these two language families account for the four most spoken languages in the world: English, Chinese Mandarin, Hindi, and Spanish.

191. (B) An urban ethnic enclave that is held together by external forces of discrimination and marginalization, as well as by internal forces of community identity and ethnic solidarity, is known as a ghetto. The term originally referred to neighborhoods in which Jewish residents were forced to live in many European cities prior to and during World War II.

192. (B) Cultural imperialism refers to one culture's dominance over another culture, often as a result of forceful control. The conquest of the Americas, during which time native inhabitants were made to adopt European cultural habits and customs, including style of dress, may be cited as an example of cultural imperialism.

193. (A) The five standard elements of mental mapping are paths, edges, districts, nodes, and landmarks. Paths refer to the linear conduits along which people move within a particular space. Paths typically represent routes for getting from place to place. Examples of paths include streets, trails, and sidewalks. Alternatively, edges refer to the linear boundaries that define the limits of a particular space. Examples of edges include fences, walls, and other types of physical barriers. Next, districts refer to thematic areas within a particular space that have a definable character or identity. Examples could include such areas as entertainment districts or recreational districts. Nodes, on the other hand, refer to important places of gathering, in which people interact or congregate. These include restaurants, busy street intersections, and city squares. Finally, landmarks refer to physical points of reference that help individuals orient themselves in a particular space. Examples of landmarks include clock towers, unusual buildings, or more subjective places where a particularly memorable event took place.

(B) Each of the five standard elements of cognitive mapping are evident in Sandra's mental representation of her community. Edges are thematically represented by the jagged, or sawtooth, lines that occur along the perimeter of the map. These edges occur along the busy highway, the dense forest, and the old cow pasture that is off limits. Paths are represented by the solid lines that link different places together within Sandra's cognitive map. These paths include Main Street as well as the smaller streets and trails that are evident in her map. Landmarks are represented by triangles, which Sandra uses to represent important points of reference in her community. These landmarks include the flagpole, the big pine tree, the place where she was stung by a bee, the castle-style house, and the middle and high schools that are visible from Sandra's own school. Sandra represents nodes with solid black circles, to indicate the places where she interacts with others on a regular basis. These include the playground, the duck pond, the bus stop, the elementary school, as well as the houses where she and her friends live. Finally Sandra represents districts with an enclosed dashed line. There are two districts in Sandra's map, one that is likely a park district and the other that is likely a school district.

(C) Cognitive maps significantly differ from more objective cartographic representations of space in several ways. First, cognitive maps are more likely to be *selectively biased*, meaning that they arbitrarily highlight the presence of certain features while completely omitting the presence of other features. For instance, in Sandra's map only the houses that are personally significant to Sandra are represented while all others are omitted. Second, cognitive maps are more likely to be *not to scale*, meaning that the relative sizes of certain features, as well as the relative distances between different features, are not consistent with their actual sizes and distances in the real world.

194. (A) The three primary kinds of cultural regions studied in human geography are formal, functional, and vernacular culture regions. Formal cultural regions are geographical areas defined by the relatively *homogeneous* presence of one or more distinct cultural traits. An area in which the majority of inhabitants share the same language, dialect, religious beliefs, ethnic identity, and/or political affiliations would constitute a formal culture region. For example, the area along the United States–Mexico border, in which the cultural traits of Spanish language and Catholic religion are common, is often referred to as a Hispanic formal culture region. Alternatively, functional cultural regions are areas defined by *functional* integrity, or the ability of the area to operate as a unified social, economic, or political unit. Examples of functional cultural regions include such territorial entities as states, counties, or cities, which have determinate boundaries inside of which certain rights, privileges, services, duties, and laws are provided. Finally, vernacular cultural regions are relatively subjective areas loosely defined according to certain popular attitudes, beliefs, or stereotypes about the cultural, historical, or physical identity of a general area. Examples of vernacular culture regions in the United States include New England in the Northeast, Dixie in the South, and Appalachia, a popular culture region that roughly corresponds to the southern part of the Appalachian Mountain chain.

(B) No single approach to classifying cultural regions is perfect, and each offers certain advantages and drawbacks. One advantage of the formal cultural region approach is that it allows geographers to measure the geographical domain or extent of *specific* cultural traits or cultural complexes. However, one drawback is that the boundaries, or extent, of a particular cultural trait or complex are rarely ever able to be absolutely determined. Rather, these boundaries may be seen to gradually fade away as one moves farther away from the core of a particular formal region. Alternatively, with respect to the functional culture region approach, one of the main advantages is that the limits or boundaries of this region *can* be defined according to where the functional unit's jurisdiction ends. However, one of the drawbacks of the functional approach is that it yields little information about cultural patterns within this purely functional system. Finally, with regard to vernacular cultural regions, one advantage is that this approach recognizes popular regional identities that already exist among culture groups. By focusing on vernacular culture regions, geographers may understand how sense of place informs inhabitants' sense of identity. However, one major disadvantage to the vernacular approach is that there is no *objective* way to measure the extent of a particular vernacular region. Instead, this type of region is subjectively defined, meaning that its perceived boundaries and location are likely to vary somewhat from person to person.

Chapter 4: The Political Organization of Space

195. (B) The physical distance between members of the same ethnic group tends to become social distance, which then causes the fragmentation of the ethnic group.

196. (A) Transnational migrants and immigrants use frequent communication, through digital devices and material culture, including letters and objects, to maintain a "human network" in multiple homelands.

197. (A) If one or both of the states have tariffs on certain goods, there is likely to be less trade between them. The presence of the tariffs tends to affect the ease of trade more than a long distance.

198. (B) The act of frequently migrating between two states demonstrates that an individual has an investment in both.

199. (B) When two states have a practice of allowing their citizens to immigrate between and work freely in both states, individuals are most likely to have fluid, or ever-changing, national identities. The lack of formality needed to cross the states' borders allows citizens of both states to have a great deal of interaction with one another.

200. (D) A federal state is the most likely state to possess multiple systems of checks and balances so that federal and localized governments do not threaten each other's powers and responsibilities.

201. (E) A state with centralized power is called a unitary state.

202. (A) A confederation, or union, between states is most likely to arise in a federal state. A federal state contains multiple states with limited powers, one of which is the opportunity to strike up an alliance.

203. (A) The development of a self-governing region has the most potential to disrupt and supplant the power of a unitary state, which has a single national governing body.

204. (D) A confederation of states that is moving toward becoming one state is most likely to attempt to govern itself through a series of agreements, signed by all parties. These agreements would be most similar to a series of treaties.

205. (B) Most of the world's unitary states are located on the continents of Africa and Asia. Unitary states include Niger, Senegal, Uganda, Zambia, Indonesia, Singapore, and Sri Lanka.

206. (C) A buffer state is thought to allow the balance of power between two major neighboring states to continue to exist.

207. (D) Today, states mainly use economic activities to seize control of waters and coastal lands that are in dispute. They use their frequent presence in the region to justify exercising jurisdiction over the territory.

208. (A) Territoriality, which involves the separation of human populations by boundaries, influences the development of different cultures.

209. (C) People divide a continent into regional trade blocs to promote economic unity between member states. The point of creating a regional trade bloc is to exclude nonmember states from preferential arrangements, thereby conferring economic advantages, and encouraging political alliances, among member states.

210. (D) A superimposed border is one that was created by an outside power or political authority without taking into account the cultural organization of the landscape—for example, the border created between North and South Korea.

211. (B) Physical boundaries of states are those that create an actual barrier and can be felt and seen, such as lakes, walls, mountains, and seas.

212. (E) Geometric boundaries are defined as political boundaries that take the form of a straight line or arc.

213. (B) Empires often posted small groups of guards or soldiers at defensive forts along borders to enforce rules of entry and exit, as well as maintain the border itself.

214. (D) Legislators and the leaders of political parties typically use the results of a census to determine the new population and ethnic makeup of regions. They then use this information to draw lines for districts that represent *communities of interest* in a fair and balanced manner.

215. (A) An allocational boundary dispute occurs when two powers disagree on the division or ownership of a resource, usually a natural resource that is present in both of their territories.

216. (A) A separation fence typically exists to show where two states have agreed their national borders should be situated as part of the terms of a cease-fire agreement. A separation fence is usually a militarized border, and crossing it without the correct documentation is seen as a hostile act.

217. (A) The collapse of large political federations revealed that states should have common economic goals to solidify connections between their governments. These goals should overcome their resistance to work together because of ethnic conflicts.

218. (D) When a nation state undergoes political turmoil, its population tends to disperse into neighboring states. This leads to the potential for more ethnic diversity in states that surround the state that is experiencing political problems if the two states have different ethnic populations.

219. (B) The act of locating environmental hazards close to regions or neighborhoods that are mainly populated by minorities, accomplished via political representation, has been termed *environmental racism*. This practice disadvantages certain groups because of their race and ethnic origin.

220. (E) A state that contains distinct environmental zones that encourage different ways of life is more likely to be home to a population that sees itself as socially and politically divided.

221. (C) Economic competition encourages political competition. A state that wants to reach the same markets and utilize the same resources as another state is most likely to develop political concerns about the actions of its competitor.

222. (C) A nation-state is typically understood to be a country in which the population is ethnically uniform, which allows for a shared language, cultural heritage, and religion.

223. (B) An Exclusive Economic Zone (EEZ) was created by the United Nations Convention on Laws of the Sea and denotes an area where a state has special rights regarding the exploration and use of resources, including minerals and marine life.

224. (D) A political leader might use popular media to push for the idea of a united, relatively homogeneous, and shared national culture. The traditional concept of a nation-state involves the population of the state having cultural solidarity and remaining resistant to change from outside.

225. (A) A nation-state is partially defined by its sovereignty. The state government's most important responsibilities include defending the state from invasion and outside rule. The state government must also prevent different populations within its borders from fragmenting the state.

226. (C) A nation-state that experiences a large influx of immigrants is the most at risk to suffer a crisis of identity, which could fragment it politically and socially.

227. (E) Nation-states tend to view the land of their state as nontransferable. The leader of a nation-state would not be likely to agree with an intergovernmental action that mandated that his or her country exchange territory with another state.

228. (C) The practice of gerrymandering involves redistricting a legislative territory to provide one party with an unequal advantage during the electoral process.

229. (C) The Arab League's acts to coordinate free trade among member states reduce each state's sovereign authority over its economic affairs.

230. (B) An empire's political fragmentation is most likely to lead to instability in frontier regions. This is what occurred as the Roman Empire declined, especially in the areas that today compose France and Germany.

231. (D) Devolution involves the distribution of powers formerly held by the central government to regional or state governments. Devolution may be temporary or can be a permanent arrangement, but the central government continues to hold most of the authority.

232. (A) Domestic and international acts of terror have the same effect: to threaten a population using violence. A terrorist act is one intended to cause panic and harm.

233. (A) Electoral geography can most effectively be studied in democratic states, in which voters can freely cast their votes for the candidate of their choice.

234. (D) Members of the Allied forces acted jointly to limit Germany's sovereign powers to prosecute Nazi war criminals. They did not feel Germany would pursue this action and punish offenders effectively.

235. (B) NATO is a military alliance, originally organized by member states to defend one another against Russia and Germany.

236. (A) The European Union is an example of supranationalism because its member states have transferred some of their powers to a central authority. The establishment and continuing stability of a central intergovernmental authority allows member states to make many decisions as a group.

237. (C) The migratory movements of survivors of a terrorist attack is a phenomenon that can be effectively mapped with geographic techniques. None of the other phenomena can be visualized effectively.

238. (A) Electoral geographers study the different ways that places and regions, and the people in them, affect the conduct and results of elections.

239. (C) The United Nations' goal is to maintain international peace. It will use economic and military sanctions to limit the sovereign powers of any state that threatens international peace.

240. (B) Australia is a union because its states are united under a common constitution and central federal government.

241. (B) Large states such as Canada have used devolution to allow populations in resource-rich areas to become more self-sufficient in exchange for a share of the resources. In Canada, the population of the Northwest Territories has gained more power to educate its residents, oversee its airports, and manage its forests.

242. (D) Democratic states that experience acts of terrorism often enact laws that limit civil liberties in an effort to prevent another attack.

243. (C) Political cleavages vary widely and can be traced to class, language, religion, culture, attitudes about national constitutions—almost any issue that particularly concerns voters.

244. (B) NGOs, such as Amnesty International, often publicize information about alleged human rights violations in attempts to limit those states' sovereign powers.

245. (A) Before the 1960s, India's caste system divided the state into a number of socially discrete groups. The continued existence of the caste system is one of the factors that caused political fragmentation within the subcontinent.

246. (B) The adjective *supranational* is indicative of more than one national government being engaged in an effort. Therefore, a supranational resolution is one that is signed by a group of different states.

247. (E) Colonists who use religion to control indigenous groups often do so with the aim of creating an environment where the groups were more hospitable to further colonization because of the shared religion.

248. (D) Spain could not maintain its control over its New World colonies. Many colonies successfully staged revolutions to gain their independence in the 19th century.

249. (C) Between the 15th and 19th centuries, European nations used chartered trading companies to engage in imperialism in India.

250. (C) Settlers from the colonizing country are most likely to allow information and revenue to flow back from the colony to the colonizing country.

251. (A) In the United States and Canada, national governments followed the doctrine of imperialism by allowing their citizens to expand the territories of these countries, while mandating that indigenous groups be relocated or remain on reservations.

252. (E) British imperialism has been the most influential type of imperialism in the past two centuries. Many other Western states have mimicked Great Britain's efforts to form a worldwide commercial and ideological empire.

253. (C) In democracies, citizens have civil liberties. A state that is transitioning from a dictatorship to a democracy must grant its citizens protection from powerful leaders who threaten civil liberties.

254. (A) The end of the Civil War brought with it a grant of voting rights to African Americans. This act caused participatory democracy in the United States to increase in the years immediately after the war ended.

255. (C) Elections must be free and open to the majority of the state's citizens to establish a democracy. If national elections are closed to certain segments of the population or are forced, the elections are less likely to establish a democratic form of government.

256. (B) Advocates of military intervention often state that Germany and Japan were able to establish themselves as democracies partly because of policing and sanctions by the international community.

257. (D) The establishment of a legislative body is an extremely common step in the process of democratization. The legislative body often serves to anchor the nation in the democratic process, providing an avenue for voters to discourage leaders who attempt to become dictators.

258. (C) Since the USSR dissolved and became a number of separate states, the majority of smaller nations that the USSR had aided strengthened their sovereign powers. If they had chosen not to do so, other states would likely have dominated them.

259. (A) An agreement between two states to grant dual citizenship to members of a certain ethnic group would be most likely to unify the ethnic group. A real-life example of this can be seen in the case of the Indian Tamils. In the 1960s, the Indian and Sri Lankan governments agreed to give Indian Tamils citizenship to Sri Lanka. There are multiple diverse communities of Tamils in India and Sri Lanka.

Yet the bonds between most of them have strengthened since Sri Lanka and India formed this agreement.

260. (B) Devolution is a dispersal of the central government's powers. Basque groups in Spain could directly force a devolution of the Spanish government by gaining political control over certain regions of the country.

261. (E) The lack of political unity among states in the Middle East makes it difficult for them to address supranational concerns, which are issues beyond the authority of a single government. An example of a supranational concern is the interest in preserving sites of cultural heritage.

262. (D) When two or more states with political differences form a federation, they must unify. The other answer choices involve processes that are not necessary to create a successful federation.

263. (C) States that want a resource that another state possesses would be most likely to try to limit the powers of the state with the resource.

264. (B) The end of the Cold War allowed electoral geographers to study political cleavages where they had not been able to before: in Poland and the Czech Republic. These nations were formerly Communist states that had been heavily influenced by the former Union of Soviet Socialist Republics (USSR).

265. (A) Louisiana now has six seats instead of seven because one area of the state, the area encompassing the city of New Orleans and its surrounding environs, was severely affected by Hurricane Katrina. The city of New Orleans was flooded and lost much of its population. Individuals relocated to other parts of the state as well as to other states. In addition, Louisiana did not experience much population growth between 2000 and 2010. The change in the number of districts affects the entire state. Louisiana will not have as much voting power, and therefore political clout, in the U.S. House of Representatives as it did in the past.

(B) The district was also extended because it contains a large number of Democratic voters. Republican candidates would not want to face a loss to a Democrat in this region. One result of including more territory in the second district is that African Americans' and Democrats' votes will be diluted. If the area of and surrounding Baton Rouge was part of another district, a Democratic candidate would have more of a chance to win a seat in another district. Another result of including more territory in the second district was pacifying both African Americans and Democrats who might have contested the redistricting plan. The extension of the district allowed African Americans to be more certain that they would retain dominance in this district. There was some concern, because the area is underpopulated. It lost a huge number of people after Hurricane Katrina, far more than many other districts. The Voting Rights Act of 1965 requires Louisiana to pass a redistricting plan that affords African Americans an equal right to be represented in Congress. A third result of the extension of the second district is the increase in partisanship between the Republican and Democratic congressmen from Louisiana. Since the extension led to the two sides eventually agreeing on the redistricting plan, the plan established some common ground between the parties.

(C) The U.S. Congress upholds and amends the statutes that make up the provisions of the Civil Rights Act of 1964. These portions of the U.S. Code make it illegal to apply voter registration requirements unequally. The U.S. Congress upholds and amends the other statutes (beyond the ones mentioned in the question) that make up the Voting Rights Act of 1965, which banned literacy tests for voters. These tests tended to have the effect of disenfranchising African American voters. The U.S. Supreme Court confronts any challenges to the 14th Amendment, which made African Americans citizens and provides all citizens the same protections under state and federal laws. The U.S. Supreme Court confronts any challenge to the 15th Amendment, which protects the voting rights of African American men. The U.S. Supreme Court confronts any challenge to the 19th Amendment, which provides women (including African Americans) with the right to vote.

266. (A) In order to protect itself from terrorism, the states of the United Kingdom could have formed a task force, with representatives from each state, to target terrorist cells across the UK. The states could have sought financial and educational help from states outside the UK to fund and train in counterterrorist activities. The states could have worked cooperatively to screen travelers and limit travel between and out of the states. The states could have engaged in negotiations and discussions with nationalist groups to solve the problems that led to agitation and violence. The states could have worked to more closely monitor and later block financial transactions between suspects and possible donors. The states could have formed a partnership with the Republic of Ireland to oppose the terrorist activities.

(B) Northern Ireland is located on the same island as the Republic of Ireland. Over the Irish Sea, and directly across from the island, lie Scotland, England, and Wales. It is only a short distance to cities that have high populations that terrorists might want to target. To facilitate the organization of terrorist activities, English is the dominant language in most of these countries. The states are also somewhat culturally similar to Northern Ireland. The Republic of Ireland and the members of the United Kingdom afford individuals a high amount of personal freedom. Individuals and families are spread across the states. The states share common banking institutions, making it easy for individuals to move money between people. The unification of the four countries of the UK can serve to make other states' political representatives into antagonists of Northern Ireland's terrorist groups. England blocks the island of Ireland from most of the European mainland. Yet from London, it is only a short distance to France, Spain, and Germany. These three states contain major cities with high populations that are cultural centers for Western Europe. These major cities are also economic engines for Western Europe. They are home to financial activities that affect areas to which they maintain governmental ties, such as the Caribbean. Two of the states, France and Spain, are home to other terrorist groups, which support Basque and Catalonian independence. Supporters of these groups might assist and defend terrorists from Northern Ireland.

(C) The allotment of additional powers to Northern Ireland has helped it to become more politically stable. The removal of British forces and security and the development of Northern Ireland forces and security have led to the creation of a task force that is more familiar with and less antagonistic toward Northern Ireland's citizens. This has led to less frustration and anger against England by groups in Northern Ireland. The terms of the Belfast Agreement require England to recognize and respect efforts by Northern Ireland to separate from the United Kingdom and move toward uniting with the Republic of Ireland. The recognition has allowed citizens of Northern Ireland to see political representation and democratic government as a road to independence. As Northern Ireland's government has become more powerful and respected, it has become more effective at reducing terrorist activity.

Chapter 5: Agriculture and Rural Land Use

267. (B) The Second Agricultural Revolution occurred from around 1750 to 1900, at the same time as the Industrial Revolution.

268. (A) The Third Agricultural Revolution is sometimes referred to as the Green Revolution.

269. (B) Locations farthest from large bodies of water, such as oceans, are more likely to experience extreme climates.

270. (D) Dogs, pigs, and chickens were first domesticated in Southeast Asia.

271. (E) Of the answer choices listed, pastoral nomadism is the only form of agriculture that is not an example of commercial agriculture.

272. (C) Crop rotation is the planting of different crops in the same field from year to year to replenish the nutrients in the soil used up by the previous crops.

273. (B) Wet rice is grown in rice sawahs planted in the sides of hills that are terraced so that water irrigates the plants but does not sit and become stagnant.

274. (D) Squash and beans were first domesticated in Mexico, the first major area of seed agriculture.

275. (E) Most ethanol produced in South America is made from sugarcane. In the United States, ethanol is made from corn.

276. (A) Market-gardening activities occur in the first zone of von Thünen's model of agricultural land use.

277. (D) Because of disorganization and lack of communication along production lines, the collectivization of agricultural production initially resulted in food shortages.

278. (E) All of the answer choices except wheat represent traditional plantation crops, typically grown in tropical locations.

279. (B) Cash-cropping is the practice of growing crops for profit, usually on a large scale. This is a form of extensive agriculture.

280. (C) Organic farming, growing crops without the use of pesticides, has grown in popularity since the ill effects of pesticides were discovered.

281. (E) Of the answer choices listed, rice is the only crop that is not grown on truck farms. Truck farming generally refers to commercial gardening and fruit farming and is called that because of a Middle English word meaning "bartering."

282. (A) The development of subsistence farming, the practice of growing all of the crops needed to sustain a community in one location, allowed people to settle permanently.

283. (D) The development of new techniques to increase farm yield, including higher-yield seeds and the expanded use of fertilizers in the latter part of the 20th century, was the beginning of the Third Agricultural Revolution, also called the Green Revolution.

284. (B) Coffee was domesticated in present-day Ethiopia about 1,200 years ago.

285. (C) The township and range system of land use divided land into square-mile tracts.

286. (A) China has a government-controlled economy, and the government dictates the types and quantities of crops grown by farmers.

287. (E) Winter wheat is planted in the fall and harvested in the subsequent summer or early fall.

288. (B) A reaper is a farm tool that harvests grains standing in the field.

289. (C) Biomass is organic matter from living, or recently living, organisms. Decomposing biomass can provide an alternative, renewable energy source.

290. (E) When herds of livestock are grazed over large areas, that is a form of commercial agriculture called ranching.

291. (A) NIMBY is an acronym for "not in my backyard"and NIMBYism occurs when residents oppose a project being built near them, even if it is necessary infrastructure such as a power plant or a new road.

292. (A) Farming on long lots involves using long fields that extend back from waterways such as rivers. Farmers along the water source use the waterways to transport their goods.

293. (E) Mediterranean agriculture requires a moderate climate with cool and wet winters. Apples are the only crops of those listed that do not grow in this climate.

294. (A) Subsistence agriculture is when farmers grow enough to feed their own families but not extra to sell or trade for other goods.

295. (A) Creative destruction occurs when the original landscape is altered, usually through the removal of vegetation, to raise crops or livestock.

296. (B) The process of agriculture that requires most work to be done by hand using manual tools is called labor-intensive farming.

297. (C) Mineral fuels are also known as fossil fuels. Natural gas, oil, and coal are examples of mineral fuels.

298. (A) The preservationist land use model involves protecting the environment through encouraging people to not alter the natural landscape, which preservationists view as more important than economic activity.

299. (B) Animal domestication refers to the process of training animals, sometimes over generations, to be comfortable around humans and to rely on humans as well as provide resources.

300. (C) The tragedy of the commons, developed by William Forest Lloyd and Garret Hardin, asserts that people will do what is in their own best interest even if it is detrimental to the common good.

301. (B) Pastoral nomadism is a type of herding that involves moving herds each season to locations that are most suitable for the animals.

302. (A) This is the only answer choice that describes a use of land in which the humans altering the landscape attempt to preserve the natural habitat.

303. (D) Shifting cultivation agriculture occupies most farmland throughout the world.

304. (A) Plantation agriculture is practiced primarily in developing countries.

305. (D) Montana is the only state listed that is not located in the Corn Belt in the midwestern United States.

306. (B) Cereal grains are the most widely grown crops in the world.

307. (D) *Kibbutzim*, which means "gathering" or "clustering" in Hebrew, is a system of voluntary collective farming in Israel. Collective or communal farming is based on group land ownership, pooled labor, and shared income. Vietnam, Hungary, Cuba, and the Soviet Union all instituted forced collective farming as part of their Communist governments.

308. (C) A feedlot is where animals are sent to fatten up prior to slaughter. They are fed high-grain diets to increase fat.

309. (B) Intertillage refers to planting between the rows of crops. A common practice in the tropics is to plant taller, stronger crops in between rows of lower, fragile crops to protect the fragile crops from downpours.

310. (B) A staple food is a primary food source that comprises the majority of the diet. Groups of people depend on staple foods for the majority of their nourishment. In Central America beans, corn (maize), potatoes, and squash are all traditional staple foods that people depend on for their dietary needs. Wheat is much more popular in the diets of people in North America and Eurasia.

311. (E) An agrarian society relies on the cultivation of land (farming). Both *municipal* and *metropolitan* refer to developed cities. Hunter-gatherer societies mainly forage for wild food instead of growing domesticated plants. A naturalist is someone who studies nature, the environment, and related earth sciences.

312. (C) The debt-for-nature swap is a program for developing countries that reduces their foreign debt and promotes local conservation funding. It is most common in the tropics, where percentages of plant and animal diversity are high.

313. (A) Mediterranean agriculture extends beyond the Mediterranean basin and also includes California, central Chile, South Africa, and southwest Australia because of their similar climates. These regions are known for their fruit crops as well as other specialized plants that can tolerate moderate rainfall in the winter season.

314. (D) Domesticated plants and animals are genetically adapted from their wild predecessors for human diets and other needs. *Feral* means "wild"; *cultivated* means "to grow"; *primitive* refers to early development; and *indigenous* means "native."

315. (B) Industrial agriculture refers to the use of machinery in modern farming. The goal of industrial agriculture is to increase food availability. There are serious environmental and social consequences such as water pollution and lack of jobs in rural farm-based communities.

316. (D) Slash-and-burn, a technique often used in tropical regions to clear forest-land for farming, is an example of subsistence farming. Subsistence farmers produce enough food to support their families but not enough for export.

317. (E) A crop grown for profit is known as a cash crop. Historically in the United States, cotton and tobacco were cash crops that brought in revenue through export.

318. (D) Market gardening produces a variety of crops on a small scale during the local growing season. Monoculture is the practice of growing one crop at a large scale for cash.

319. (D) Desertification is the process of fertile land turning into desert as a result of poor environmental and social management. Overgrazing, off-road vehicle use, and overcultivation all contribute to soil loss. Poor irrigation can also cause problems, such as salinization, which degrades the soil. Policies that favor nomadic herding over sedentary farming decrease the tendency toward desertification because nomadic herders can more easily move and adjust to climate and resource availabilities.

320. (B) Mining for copper and other natural resources from the ground are examples of the extractive industry. Forestry, fishing, agriculture, and animal husbandry are not part of the extractive industry.

321. (C) Carl Sauer, a geographer from University of California, Berkeley, argued that natural landscapes had been indirectly altered by human activity. He also wrote on plant and animal domestication and determined that plant domestication first originated in hilly areas with sedentary people.

322. (A) A suitcase farm is a commercial farm where no one lives and that is farmed by migratory workers. It is common in the United States with commercial grain agriculture.

323. (E) The agricultural location model, identified by Johann Heinrich von Thünen, explains where specific agriculture activities should be located to maximize profit. Dairying and vegetable farms should be closest to the central market due to the short travel distance that prevents crops from spoiling. Timber and firewood should be the next closest to the market, as they are needed to build homes and for fuel. Additionally, wood is difficult to transport, so production near the city is beneficial. Grain crops should be grown beyond the timber and firewood area, since the grain will not spoil during transportation. Finally, ranching should occur at the outermost level, closest to the wilderness, since animals can transport themselves to the market. Von Thünen argued that farmers who do not utilize the location model will go bankrupt from lack of profits.

324. (A) The metes and bounds system was primarily used east of the Appalachian Mountains and relies on descriptions of land ownership and the position of natural features such as streams. It was abandoned because of its imprecise nature.

325. (D) Aquaculture is the farming and cultivation of fish and shellfish such as oysters. Polyculture is farming multiple crops, while monoculture is reliance on a single crop. Hydroponics is the practice of cultivating plants in a nutrient-rich water, and aeroponics cultivates plants where roots are in the open air. Waterlogging refers to soil that is saturated by groundwater and cannot support agriculture.

326. (C) A farm crisis, such as the one that occurred in the United States in the 1980s, is the result of mass crop production that supplies more food than is in demand. This overproduction leads to lower prices of crops, resulting in less profit for farmers. Small family farms are less able to cope with the loss of profit than large commercial farms; therefore, the number of small farms has decreased.

327. (A) Crop rotation is the practice of planting different types of crops in a field each season. This practice helps replenish nutrients in the soil. Companion cropping and succession cropping are types of double cropping, where two crops are planted in the same field in one growing season. No-till planting does not till the land after a harvest to reduce soil erosion.

328. (B) Sustainable yield refers to natural capital and is the amount of a natural material, animal, or plant that can be extracted without depleting the natural capital.

329. (D) Luxury crops are items that are not necessary for survival and typically are sold at higher prices. Wool is the only answer choice that does not fit this description.

330. (D) The growing season is the period during the year that a plant can grow. In general, growing seasons near the equator are longer than near the poles because the equator receives more sunlight. Growing seasons also can be influenced by climate patterns and wind or ocean currents.

331. (B) The Green Revolution uses hybrid seeds that produce higher yields of food, which has prevented food crises in some regions. The seeds have to be purchased each year, as they cannot reproduce themselves. Also, large quantities of pesticides and fertilizers must be used to ensure seed success. The expense of seeds, pesticides, and fertilizers does not allow poor farmers to profit from farming, and social inequalities still prevail in many of the developing countries where this type of farming has been implemented since the 1970s.

332. (C) Agribusiness is any practice related to food production, from the farm to the market to the consumer.

333. (A) The enclosure movement changed farming in England during the 18th century by consolidating the many small farms into fewer large farms.

334. (C) Carl Sauer mapped the agriculture origins (or hearths) of domestic plants and animals. He identified central and northwest South America, western Africa, and Southeast Asia as the primary hearths of domestication.

335. (E) The Fertile Crescent is one of the regions where sedentary farming first started. Sedentary farming led to the development of cities and cultures.

336. (B) Chronologically, pastoralism, which arose in the Neolithic period, most closely followed hunting and gathering.

337. (D) One of the benefits of crop rotation is that the need for artificial fertilizers is reduced by the planting of complementary crops.

338. (A) Feedlots, in which large numbers of animals are raised in a small area, are an example of intensive cultivation.

339. (C) The lack of synthetic pesticides on organic farms produces more diverse ecosystems than can be found on conventional farms, which is an environmental benefit.

340. (E) All of the other statements are true of the von Thünen model, but according to Von Thünen, forests were optimally located in the second ring of his land use model.

341. (C) Of all the choices, C best characterizes the complex legacy of the Green Revolution.

342. (A) The British Agricultural Revolution displaced a number of agricultural workers as a result of enclosure and mechanization, which led to a ready labor force for the growing factory system during the Industrial Revolution.

343. (D) Intensive cultivation at the subsistence level is practiced in many areas of the world, particularly in Asia.

344. (A) There is ample evidence that fruit trees were grown alongside cereal crops from the Neolithic era, just as agriculture was beginning.

345. (B) Transhumance is the seasonal, vertical movement of livestock for grazing, usually from summer pastures at higher elevation to winter pastures at lower elevation.

346. (A) The First Agricultural Revolution is known as the Neolithic Revolution and represents the transition from hunting and gathering to the farming of domesticated plants. The domestication of plants and animals allowed permanent settlements to form in place of nomadic groups. Sedentary societies led to more complex economies and allowed the development of arts, sciences, and culture.

(B) The Second Agricultural Revolution occurred between 1750 and 1900 in the developed world. New machinery, such as Eli Whitney's cotton gin, helped farmers work more land with the same amount of labor. Food production increased as a result. New crop rotations were implemented to produce better yields, and new plant hybrids were developed based on breeding experiments. As transportation improved, crops and other goods were more easily transported to markets before spoiling. As a result of the increase in machinery on the farms, more people left the farms to work in urban areas that needed factory workers.

(C) The Third Agricultural Revolution represents modern commercial agriculture starting around the 1960s. Primary, secondary, and tertiary farming activities blended during the Third Revolution. Mechanization also increased, as well as the development of hybridization technologies to increase crop yields, which led to increases in food yields but also impacted traditional social and economic systems as well as the environment.

347. (A) Some factors leading to desertification are overuse of water, thereby reducing water tables and draining aquifers; salinization of soils; erosion of topsoil through floods or natural disasters; tree blight, such as oak wilt disease; changing river systems due to human consumption of water; overuse of cropland, leaving it sterile and susceptible to insect infestation; and drought conditions brought on by changing global weather patterns, such as El Niño.

(B) Salinization begins when salts and chemicals from fertilizers and factory wastes build up in the soil, gradually causing it to become sterile and leading to desertification.

(C) Soil conservation can preserve and actually renew the viability of cropland. This in turn can support the animals who feed on the crops, leading to increased production of food sources, not only for humans but for all the creatures in the food web. When soils are healthy and not overused, they can sustain crops that could not grow in poorer soils, thereby leading to sustainable agriculture.

348. (A) Genetically engineered crops can benefit humans by increasing production of such staples as corn, soybeans, and orange juice and by decreasing the amount of produce lost to bacteria and insects.

(B) Possible drawbacks to genetic modification of food crops are (1) unforeseen effects on wildlife who feed on the crops, (2) possible alienation of pollinator insects like bees and butterflies (bee colony collapse may be due in part to ignorance of the effects of modifying genetic codes), and (3) destruction of said food crops because the balance of nature is out of sync, and nature cannot rebound against human manipulations on the genetic level.

(C) The future of biotechnology in relation to food crops is uncertain. While genetic engineering is widely in place already, a backlash has begun to take hold in the consciences of many people. Farmers can benefit from robust crops for a few years, then begin to see production fall off because of ecological changes caused by the manipulations they espoused. Genetically modified plants may be resistant to some blights, only to be struck down by new predators let in by the vacuum created. There is no doubt that humans will continue to manipulate gene coding. However, organic farming is gaining in popularity as a result of increased awareness among consumers of the uncertain effects of genetic modification.

Chapter 6: Industrialization and Economic Development

349. (E) All of the regions listed except northern Africa were engaged in heavy industry following the Industrial Revolution.

350. (E) Mining is a resource-based economic activity. All of the other answer choices include service-based economic activities.

351. (A) Most, but not all, export-processing zones are located in periphery and semi-periphery regions of developing nations to attract foreign investment. Mexico's system of maquiladoras on the United States–Mexico border is an example of export-processing zones.

352. (B) When companies engaged in heavy industry began to move operations to locations with lower production costs, Great Britain experienced deindustrialization.

353. (A) Rostow's stages of development assume that all countries will eventually pass through each of the five stages of economic development in a linear manner, including traditional society, preconditions for takeoff, takeoff, the drive to maturity, and the age of high mass consumption. The colonial legacy is not accounted for in Rostow's theory, which is one common criticism of it. In the second stage, there are several preconditions that demonstrate that a country is ready for takeoff, including the development of infrastructure and foreign trade relations, but foreign investment is not one of them. The fifth and final stage is the age of high mass consumption, not deindustrialization. When that can occur in a highly developed country it is not part of Rostow's theory.

354. (C) South Africa is the only country listed that is not included in the periphery.

355. (A) The Rust Belt is an industrial area that runs through the northeastern United States, dipping down into the Mid-Atlantic states and part of the Midwest. Buffalo, Detroit, and Cleveland are located in the Rust Belt.

356. (D) Maquiladoras are towns in Mexico where U.S. companies have factories, taking advantage of lower production costs. These towns are located close to the United States–Mexico border.

357. (A) The demographic transition model represents the transition of a country from high birth and death rates to low birth and death rates as the country moves through stages of economic development. China's one-child policy has greatly slowed the birth rate, so China is far ahead of other newly industrialized countries in terms of demographic transition.

358. (B) Tourism brings cash into a country when individuals from foreign countries come in and spend money on goods and services within the country.

359. (C) Fifth-world countries are characterized by a lack of a formal government. Somalia is an example of a fifth-world country.

360. (A) Offshore financial centers, such as those located in the Bahamas and Switzerland, are designed to promote business interactions and offer lower taxes and tariffs. This is attractive to companies and individuals who deal in large sums of money.

361. (D) Just-in-time manufacturing is a process of inventory management that has companies keeping just what they need on hand.

362. (D) Second-world countries are characterized by a hard-line Communist government. Of the countries listed, Cuba is the only second-world country.

363. (A) In 1997, a banking collapse in South Korea triggered an economic crisis across Asia. This led to deindustrialization in countries like South Korea and Japan.

364. (B) NAFTA stands for North American Free Trade Agreement. This agreement eased restrictions on trade between Canada, the United States, and Mexico.

365. (A) Immanuel Wallerstein theorized that the modern network of countries engaged in trade and competition emerged when European nations began exploring the rest of the world.

366. (C) Goods are classified as durable or nondurable based on the amount of time a product can be used. Durable goods are those that can be used for three years; the use of nondurable goods is limited to under a year.

367. (E) OPEC stands for Organization of the Petroleum Exporting Countries. It is the only acronym listed that does not signify a trade agreement. NAFTA refers to the North America Free Trade Agreement that created a trilateral trade bloc in North America. SADC stands for the Southern African Development Community, which works toward integrating the economies of Southern Africa, including creating a free trade area. G-3 was a trade agreement among Mexico, Venezuela, and Colombia, although Venezuela later withdrew. CEFTA refers to the Central European Free Trade Agreement, which is a trade agreement among non-European Union nations.

368. (B) Quaternary economic activities are primarily concerned with information sharing and development. Research and development is the only quaternary activity listed.

369. (A) The Human Development Index (HDI) is used by the United Nations to measure human welfare in a country. The HDI is calculated using a formula that takes into account social indicators as well as economic production.

370. (B) Alternative energy sources, such as hydropower and solar energy, are generally more expensive to produce than fossil fuels.

371. (E) Service and high-tech industry jobs do not generally result in a shorter workweek. Each of the other benefits listed are enjoyed by many in service and high-tech industries.

372. (C) Deglomeration is the movement of economic activity away from an area of previous concentration. This occurs when the market becomes overloaded with businesses providing the same services or goods.

373. (A) The Gini coefficient is a measure of the inequality of distribution of income or wealth in a country, measuring the gap between the wealthiest and poorest populations.

374. (C) A bulk-reducing industry is one in which the final product has less volume than its inputs. Steel production is the only bulk-reducing industry listed in the answer choices.

375. (A) Italy and Kuwait both have a high GNP and low gender equity. These countries have low gender equity because of social barriers to higher income and wealth for women.

376. (D) China is the only country listed in the answer choices that is not an Old Asian Tiger.

377. (A) Following World War II, the United States and Great Britain invested in the Old Asian Tiger countries, such as Japan and South Korea, to stop the spread of communism in Asia.

378. (C) The break-of-bulk point is the point along a transport route where goods must be transferred from one mode of transport to another.

379. (A) Natural gas is the only nonrenewable energy source listed in the answer choices.

380. (E) Foreign development aid given to developing countries by developed countries usually comes in the form of cash and is not expected to be paid back by the receiving country.

381. (C) Sierra Leone is a developing country that has experienced an economic crisis due to civil war and is now classified as at a lower stage of development.

382. (D) As industry moves out of first-world countries, industrial countries such as the United States and Great Britain have seen a decline in industry.

383. (D) One of the principles of Fordism was to eliminate the need for skilled labor in manufacturing and increase the unskilled labor force. Ford wanted to pay unskilled laborers higher wages to ensure that they could purchase the automobiles they were producing.

384. (E) Workers cannot be forced to join a union as a condition of employment in a right-to-work state.

385. (B) A cottage industry is one in which the manufacturing of goods takes place in the home.

386. (A) The Mid-Atlantic region of the United States is known as a megalopolis, or a large metropolitan area that extends through a chain of connecting cities.

387. (B) The former Soviet Union lost most of its agricultural activity and coal deposits to Ukraine when the Soviet Union was dissolved.

388. (C) One of the world's largest industrial parks is located in Shanghai, China.

389. (C) In Socialist economies the government controls the prices of basic goods and services, including energy and transportation, to prevent prices from being too high, thereby ensuring that everyone can afford to pay for these essential services.

390. (B) Dependency theory asserts some countries do nothing to address high poverty rates in order to keep an elite ruling class in power, which controls all of the country's economic resources.

391. (A) According to the core-periphery model, areas in a downward transition have high unemployment rates.

392. (B) According to Richard Nolan's stages of growth model, technology begins to spread during the contagion stage.

393. (E) The Sunbelt, located in the U.S. South and parts of the Southwest, is in upward transition according to the core-periphery model.

394. (B) Money left after all necessary bills have been paid is called expendable income.

395. (A) The technology gap refers to the gap in access to and knowledge about technology. Poorer populations have less access to technology, and younger people tend to know more about how to use technology than older people, for example.

396. (C) Under the core-periphery model, the northern part of Alaska that contains crude oil is classified as a resource frontier.

397. (C) Special economic zones (SEZs) offer incentives for foreign businesses. In China, many foreign companies have established headquarters in these SEZs.

398. (A) The idea that an abundance of both fossil fuels and alternative energy is available throughout the world and that these resources can be shared is the fundamental principle of the optimistic viewpoint of economic development.

399. (D) Standard of living is the level of wealth and personal enjoyment that a person experiences, which can be measured in several ways, including the average real gross domestic product per capita.

400. (D) In many countries in sub-Saharan Africa, life expectancy reaches only 50 years. This is the lowest of the regions listed.

401. (C) A basic industry is one in which most of the goods or services produced are exported out of the geographical region. Computer equipment manufacturing is the basic industry in the Silicon Valley in California.

402. (E) Boston, located in the Mid-Atlantic region, is the only city listed not found in the Eastern Great Lakes region.

403. (B) The Physical Quality of Life Index is a measurement calculated using literacy rate, life expectancy, and infant mortality.

404. (C) The gross domestic product is a measure of the total goods and services produced by a country. The gross domestic product per capita is this measurement divided by the country's total population.

405. (C) Of the modes of transportation listed, ships are the most energy efficient per mile of travel.

406. (C) Shopping malls are an example of agglomeration, the concentration of firms offering similar goods and services.

407. (A) Brain drain occurs when young people leave their home country to obtain an education superior to the one they could obtain in their home country and do not return.

408. (A) At the end of World War II, Japan signed a treaty stating that it would not build its military. This allowed the Japanese government to invest in industrial development, and Japan soon became a world leader in industry.

409. (D) E-commerce transactions are expected to increase their rapid growth over the next decade as more and more people gain access to high-speed Internet and smartphone technology.

410. (A) A free-trade zone, or export processing zone, is an area where trade laws of a country such as tariffs, bureaucratic requirements, and quotas are eliminated in hopes of stimulating foreign trade and industry.

411. (E) The Industrial Revolution started in Great Britain and spread at varying speeds throughout the rest of the world, mostly in the 19th century.

412. (E) A footloose industry is one that can be located anywhere without ramifications from resources or transportation. Examples include call centers and many high-tech industries.

413. (C) Of these choices, the only one that speaks to the utility of GDP as a measure of standard of living is its consistency as a worldwide measure of economic activity.

414. (D) One of the most serious criticisms of the HDI is that it does not consider ecological and environmental factors.

415. (E) They are far more likely to live in overcrowded, squalid, and unsanitary conditions. Often the poor in rural areas fare better because there is less overcrowding and competition for resources in rural areas.

416. (A) The countries of Europe used their advantages to dominate the semiperipheral and peripheral countries and lands of the time.

417. (B) Industries with material orientation rely on raw materials for their existence and thus are most advantageously located near those materials. Many of these industries involve the extraction of resources.

418. (E) Least cost theory does not take consumer demand into account.

419. (E) Globalization has affected different countries and areas of the world in different ways and has not spread across the globe at a uniform rate.

420. (D) One of the biggest criticisms of ecotourism is that it can sometimes cause the displacement of indigenous peoples to enhance the ecotourism experience. The Masai in East Africa are a prime example of an indigenous culture displaced for the purposes of ecotourism.

421. (A) The mechanization of agriculture during the Agricultural Revolution helped provide surplus workers for British factories during this period.

422. (B) While all of the other choices are true, not all areas of the globe have equal access to the benefits of technology.

423. (D) Under the balanced growth approach to economic development, also called the self-sufficiency model, a state attempts to spread investment throughout all of its regions equally.

424. (B) For many industries, situation factors can make it better for a factory to be close to the final market. Those include bulk-gaining industries, where weight is added to a product during production, such as cars and bottled beverages; single-market industries, where there is only a limited area where the product is needed; and industries like dairy production, where the end product is perishable. For industries such as copper production, however, the end product weighs much less than the raw materials used to make it, so it is more advantageous to be near the source of raw materials rather than the market.

425. (C) NAFTA does not give maquiladoras tax-exempt status in Mexico.

426. (B) A bulk-gaining industry produces products that are heavier after assembly.

427. (A) Europeans withheld advances in shipping, communications, and technology from nonmember countries so that they could retain domination of those societies.

(B) Countries like Spain, Greece, and Mexico are experiencing rapid growth in industries that languished before global communication because they can compete globally, not just locally.

(C) Semiperipheral countries got to be the aggressors and pass on the exploitation practiced on them by core countries, withholding from peripherals even their limited access to the core. This perpetuated a system of degradation and exploitation that continues to this day in much of the world.

428. (A) Cottage industries can compete with multinationals by building up a local patronage based on the idea that buying locally produced items will bring back manufacturing to communities devastated by the export of jobs overseas.

(B) Home-based businesses benefit their communities by taking commuters off the highways, reducing their carbon footprint by producing less waste than large companies, and creating a reduction in the need for large office spaces in favor of more green zones, like parks and forests.

(C) When a cottage industry outgrows its original parameters, it can be very difficult to employ conservation techniques. Burt's Bees has managed to do so by keeping its original headquarters and basing its expansion in areas that favor green practices. Another example of such companies are specialty beverage companies, like Texas Sweet Teas, which find that being green and growing their companies are a matter of making careful choices about manufacturing principles, local ingredients, clean factories, water reclamation, low carbon footprints, and local distribution networks. They can be successful in competitive markets without sacrificing their small-company ideals.

Chapter 7: Cities and Urban Land Use

429. (B) For many decades, and today in certain areas, urban areas excluded women because they provided women with fewer opportunities to work and take control of property.

430. (B) City planners are working to make cities healthier by designing neighborhoods and streets that allow urban residents to get exercise on a regular basis.

431. (A) Under the bid rent theory, land users will compete and pay higher prices for land that is more accessible to the city center.

432. (B) Hoyt's sector model theorized that low-income populations are most likely to live next to transportation corridors, such as rail lines. In a futuristic version of his model, low-income populations would be most likely to live next to high-speed rail lines.

433. (A) The gravity model of migration assumes that cities have a greater power to attract people when they are located close to one another. Derived from Newton's law of gravity, it states that having two cities located close together can improve the movement between them, and can mathematically predict the interactions between residents of the two cities based on their relative populations and distance from each other.

434. (C) Residents of edge cities and suburban areas have long relied on automobiles and public transportation to get to jobs in large cities.

435. (E) A greenbelt policy is meant to encourage a city to remake its core into a livable space.

436. (E) The political powers of a city council are most often found in the constitution of the state in which the city is located.

437. (D) In the United States, an increase in the amount of money in an urban ghetto typically results in the ghetto becoming more ethnically diverse, less segregated, and less cohesive.

438. (A) The number of senior citizens in cities, most belonging to the baby boom generation, is expected to more than double in the next quarter century.

439. (B) Landless residents usually work to improve their situations by meeting in political demonstrations and later forming grassroots organizations.

440. (D) An urban heat island is a city that is hotter than surrounding suburban or rural areas. In urban heat islands, air quality is comparatively lower and there are greater health risks due to heat waves.

441. (E) The exodus of middle- and high-income residents from urban areas to the suburbs during the 1970s and 1980s was characterized as a racial movement: "white flight."

442. (C) Housing cooperatives offer property for rent or ownership that is often owned by the cooperative and controlled equally by all residents.

443. (A) Opponents of *automobile dependency* believe that drivers of automobiles are always going to demand bigger, more streamlined roads. This reduces a city's ability to plan other types of transportation effectively.

444. (C) Many cities attempt to ensure that they contain affordable places to live and work to promote the spread of the arts and creative jobs.

445. (B) Residents of gated communities are understood to have high incomes and privileged lifestyles.

446. (A) The separation of housing and commercial zones created dead spaces in many American cities.

447. (E) Under the concentric zone model, many urban residents chose to move away from the central business district at the center of the city because it is seen as an undesirable place to live.

448. (D) A city fit the multiple-nuclei model if it had no central business district and contained a variety of different industries in different areas.

449. (C) Many European nations built public housing in efficient, yet unattractive modern apartment blocks to house returning refugees and those who had lost their homes to bombing and looting.

450. (D) In the past, many cities failed to create easy ways for people to walk and bike throughout the cities.

451. (A) Urban residents cannot be denied any of the opportunities in the answer choices except the opportunity to enter into financial agreements to solidify home ownership.

452. (E) A rise in the number of high-wage jobs in the suburbs often corresponds with a rise in the number of low-wage jobs in the central city.

453. (B) Many of the megacities of tomorrow are actually multiple cities that are growing toward one another with the promise that they will become one densely populated urban area.

454. (C) In many developing nations, rural migrants travel to the country's large cities to find employment.

455. (B) Central place theory came to be seen as inaccurate as theorists revealed that a city's place within a network of other cities determined its importance more than the city's size and its position in relation to less developed areas that surrounded it.

456. (A) Copenhagen, Denmark, is a primate city because it has the highest population of any metropolitan area in the country. It is also the cultural center of the nation.

457. (E) Since the 1980s, decentralization has increased as developers have chosen to build suburbs and edge cities that are not close to central cities.

458. (C) The city of Jerusalem has at least two central business districts to serve at least two different ethnic and religious populations, these being its Jewish and Arab populations.

459. (D) Alexandria, Egypt, was a center for learning, as evidenced by its magnificent library and considerable commercial activity.

460. (C) Christaller's central place theory assumes that perfect competition exists because all consumers are of the same income and shop in the same way.

461. (B) The rank-size rule describes the distribution of cities in a country or region. It states that a country or region has a city that is the largest, in terms of population, and other cities decrease in population compared to the largest city. The rank-size rule does not hold if you consider all of the cities in a given country or region.

462. (C) The commuter zone is the outermost ring of the concentric zone model. In this zone, residents living in outlying areas commute into the city to work and engage in activities.

463. (A) Cities that wish to reenergize inactive central business districts should take steps to draw people to the district, to encourage them to live and work there.

464. (E) The job of an individual who works as part of a municipal council is to make sure that the city government is run correctly.

465. (B) The practice of redlining involved banks and other lending institutions, including the federal government, outlining minority and low-income neighborhoods in red. These lending institutions then failed to provide affordable home loans to individuals in those neighborhoods.

466. (C) The sector model, developed in 1939, proposed that cities expand outward along major lines of transportation such as railroads because the railroads would then carry in residents who worked in the city center to their jobs during the day and back out to their homes at night.

467. (B) When a large city experiences a sudden spike in internal immigration, new residents of the city are likely to be individuals from rural areas and smaller cities, especially those that surround the large city.

468. (A) Green building is a form of gentrification because it causes the value of the environmentally friendly property, as well as other properties in the neighborhood, to increase. The increase in value defines the effect of the construction or restoration as gentrification.

469. (D) During the Neolithic Revolution, the majority of cities arose in areas where the population had found methods to generate an agricultural surplus. All of the other actions were not common among the majority of cities.

470. (E) Peasants who had been subjected to a life of economic servitude chose to abandon agricultural work in favor of factory work.

471. (A) In the earliest cities, growth and increasingly complex political organization appear to be linked to established, powerful family networks.

472. (C) Overcrowding in urban areas is a common occurrence when the rate of incoming migrants exceeds the ability of builders and city officials to create available housing.

473. (C) A large number of the earliest cities used their status as religious centers to draw crowds of pilgrims, and their donations, to sacred sites and regular rituals.

474. (B) The sale of agricultural harvests was one of the few steady sources of income for those who lived in the city or near its borders. The sale of agricultural harvests came to be seen as a source of income by political leaders as well.

475. (D) Rural-urban migration is primarily linked to economic demands. Agriculture is a seasonal activity that allows rural residents to leave for periods of time when their land must lie fallow or the harvest is over.

476. (C) Air pollution, as well as other forms of pollution, is a health risk to urban residents. Some of the other answer choices may be issues that affect modern megacities, but they are not problems.

477. (E) The defining feature of a global city is its role in international business.

478. (C) Global cities usually see low-income minority populations frequently move between neighborhoods in an effort to remain where housing and commercial space are priced affordably.

479. (B) When a city draws residents out to suburbs, residential areas within the city tend to become less cohesive and united. This causes cities to become more disorganized and leads to decentralization and urban sprawl.

480. (C) The rank-size rule holds that the nth largest city of a country will be $1/n$th the size of the largest city. Many countries contain cities that are not much smaller than the largest city. The size of the smaller cities provides an exception to the premise of the rank-size rule.

481. (D) Central place theory focuses on the mapping of market areas and the patterns through which people consume goods and services. Christaller's central place theory requires that cities be understood in relation to the markets that they serve. These are illustrated in diagrams as lattices that surround the cities.

482. (D) Edge cities tend to spring up near transportation corridors that allow people to easily commute to nearby cities or travel to faraway cities.

483. (D) John R. Borchert developed a theory that there are five different periods in the growth of American cities related to transportation technology. The five epochs are: Sail-Wagon Epoch; Iron Horse Epoch; Steel Rail Epoch; Auto-Air-Amenity Epoch; and High-Technology Epoch

484. (E) The level of desire or need of consumers to purchase a good determines how far they will travel to purchase it.

485. (C) The gravity model has been criticized because it appears static and cannot easily be modified to show how flow patterns evolve.

486. (B) The sizes of the rings in the concentric zone model are based on people's demand for land that exists within and outside of the central business district.

487. (E) Hoyt's model for the growth of cities tends to work when applied to British cities, which grew outward from a central business district along major roads and rail lines.

488. (D) Harris and Ullman came up with the multiple-nuclei model in the 1940s. At that point in time, many people within cities had begun to use cars to navigate cities more freely.

489. (A) The simplest form of the gravity model assumes that the interaction between two towns is proportionate to the product of their populations divided by the square of the distance between them.

490. (C) Suburban downtowns are nuclei independent of the central business district and have the power to draw residents that live throughout the greater metropolitan area.

491. (E) Cities want to motivate employers to create service jobs to replace industrial and manufacturing jobs that have moved to suburban or rural areas.

492. (B) Job sprawl typically involves the migration of jobs into areas within city limits and less than 15 miles from downtown.

493. (E) In central place theory, the point at which it becomes economically feasible to offer certain services is called the threshold.

494. (C) As industrial jobs have left American cities, many working-class neighborhoods have become ghettos.

495. (B) Public housing is typically offered by local, state, and federal government agencies.

496. (E) Housing in edge cities is typically private and designed so that a person feels as if he or she is in a well-tended yet lush semirural landscape.

497. (A) A road network is the most flexible transportation system, as it easily allows people to build and expand on existing routes.

498. (D) Many U.S. cities develop emergency transit plans that assist urban residents in evacuating areas of the city that have been affected by a natural disaster.

499. (A) Mexico City is in south central Mexico and is not extremely close to its major coastal ports. It is farther south than many of the country's more populated cities and northeast of the Yucatan Peninsula's most visited tourist areas. The capital city cannot be a central node in the national commodity chain for goods that travel elsewhere because of its awkward central, landlocked location. Mexico City can continue to be somewhat of a hub because it has a huge population and is a destination point for many goods. It can also serve as a checkpoint and redistribution center for goods being transported by truck from the south.

(B) Houston and San Antonio are both business centers in Texas. Houston is home to the headquarters of a number of energy, biomedical, and aeronautics industries. San Antonio is home to many health-care and financial services industries. Houston and San Antonio draw consultants and professionals from Mexico City interested in linking these industries in Mexico and the United States. Houston and San Antonio are also tourist destinations. They have high populations. They attract labor and visitors from Mexico City. This creates growing markets for Mexican products and services.

(C) Mexico City has a high number of educated professionals. It is home to many individuals who exhibit talent in business. These individuals are working to expand North American, Mexican, and Central American corporations and markets. Mexico City's size and location between the United States and the countries of Central America make it a natural center for banking and other industries that act to develop national economies, such as energy and tourism. Mexico City also has a huge labor pool, which allows it to be a source of labor as well as a center for training and industrial production. Many states in Mexico are far more rural and have less urban and industrial infrastructure than Mexico City. Some of Mexico's tourist areas are not suitable for either development or conducting and coordinating production and trade. This makes Mexico City one of the better cities in which to do business in Mexico. Mexico City further has a historic role as the nation's center for administration and business. Many industries and professionals choose not to relocate industrial, trade, and financial activity from Mexico City. They want to maintain a presence in this active, interconnected area.

500. (A) Single-parent families need housing that is economical and located near public transportation centers and schools. Single-parent families also need housing that is close to parks and shopping centers or marketplaces. Aging seniors must have housing that is close to hospitals and shopping centers so that they can obtain health services and food without cars. Aging seniors may also need blocks of connected housing broken up by parks and green spaces. This allows them to socialize with people in their age group without using cars and to remain physically active. Single individuals with service-sector jobs need housing that is located close to their places of employment and near public transportation centers. Single individuals must have housing that is economical. Units can be smaller than units for families.

(B) A city government could institute or raise sales taxes on gas. A city could raise the prices of city services, such as utilities. A city could also hold events that charge admission to generate revenue, such as expositions for different industries, or festivals, for which vendors would be required to pay fees. A city could raise its fines for zoning code violations. A city could require industries that want to locate to the city to pay a fee to build parking lots in open space.

(C) Failing to build enough affordable housing in a large metropolitan area acts to stratify the city. Rich people and poor people tend to congregate in clumps instead of being interspersed. This tends to make the city more of a fragmented collection of neighborhoods. The city grows away from being a cohesive, united, uniform area. Poorer individuals tend to move outside the city. This makes it difficult to find cheap labor for needed service industries. Not providing enough affordable housing concentrates pollution in areas where transportation corridors are most active, and it acts to clog up traffic. Commercial activity, political activity, and environmental improvement are uncommon in the most disadvantaged neighborhoods. If there is no money flowing into a neighborhood, there is a danger of it becoming a dead zone. A city with many dead zones is uninteresting and a dangerous place in which to travel. It may lose residents and business.